Repotting Your Life

Sense When You're Stuck.
Explore What's Possible.
Claim Room to Grow.

FRANCES EDMONDS

THE EXPERIMENT

NEW YORK

REPOTTING YOUR LIFE: *Sense When You're Stuck. Explore What's Possible. Claim Room to Grow.*
Copyright © 2021 by Frances Edmonds

Originally published in Great Britain by Elliott & Thompson, Ltd., in 2021. First published in North America in revised form by The Experiment, LLC, in 2022. Published by arrangement with Elliott & Thompson, Ltd.

The Experiment, LLC
220 East 23rd Street, Suite 600
New York, NY 10010-4658
theexperimentpublishing.com

THE EXPERIMENT and its colophon are registered trademarks of The Experiment, LLC. Many of the designations used by manufacturers and sellers to distinguish their products are claimed as trademarks. Where those designations appear in this book and The Experiment was aware of a trademark claim, the designations have been capitalized.

The Experiment's books are available at special discounts when purchased in bulk for premiums and sales promotions as well as for fundraising or educational use. For details, contact us at info@theexperimentpublishing.com

Library of Congress Cataloging-in-Publication Data available upon request

ISBN 978-1-61519-871-9
Ebook ISBN 978-1-61519-872-6

Cover design by Beth Bugler
Text design by Marie Doherty

Manufactured in the United States of America

First printing April 2022
10 9 8 7 6 5 4 3 2 1

*Dedicated to all my friends
at the Distinguished Careers Institute, Stanford:
a true fellowship of repotters*

Repotting, that's how you get new
bloom . . . you should have a plan of
accomplishment and when that is achieved
you should be willing to start off again.

ERNEST C. ARBUCKLE, FORMER DEAN OF THE
STANFORD GRADUATE SCHOOL OF BUSINESS, 1958–68

CONTENTS

INTRODUCTION

Few occasions are celebrated with such unalloyed optimism as the christening or naming ceremony of a baby. Some time ago, I was privileged to attend one such event and to witness the introduction of a miraculous little girl to her ecstatically grateful extended family. I use the adjective *miraculous* because without the modern miracle of IVF this particular little girl would never have been born. Events designed to mark life's major transitions, those time-honored rites of passage such as christenings, weddings, funerals, and milestone birthdays, often serve as catalysts for reflection for those present. And so it was, as the ceremony progressed and I took my turn as godmother to cuddle the new baby, that I began to consider how lucky this little girl was to be born in an era when she may well live to celebrate her hundredth birthday and to enjoy an extra thirty years of lifespan compared with a child born a century ago.

Lucky or cursed? As I started to imagine the course of this fledgling centurion's life, my optimism became tinged with apprehension. Nowadays, we are all experiencing the seismic changes precipitated by innovations in such fields as information technology and artificial intelligence. What impact might hitherto undreamed-of advances in hitherto unheard-of areas have on the way this child will have to organize her hundred years? The idea that we might have a job for life has already been relegated to the list of quaintly idiosyncratic expectations shared by previous generations, and our extended life expectancy has rendered the traditional three-phase "Learn—Earn—Retire" model obsolete. The problem we now confront is that society has yet to come up with either an alternative template or the culture and institutions necessary to negotiate the additional phases of our elongated lives. As Carl Jung famously observed way back at the start of the twentieth century, there are no "colleges for forty-year-olds that prepare them for their coming life and its demands as the ordinary colleges introduce our young people to a knowledge of the world and of life." Until communities across the world create solutions, we must rely on our own devices to come up with the answer.

My goddaughter slumbered on, blissfully unaware of the powerful forces at work around her, a modern-day Sleeping Beauty. If only, I mused, like the fairy godmother of the

Grimms' celebrated fairy tale, I could grant her some gift to help her negotiate the vagaries and vicissitudes of an increasingly volatile twenty-first century. Contemporary readers may raise a wry smile when they consider the gifts deemed desirable by the Grimms' bevvy of fairy godmothers: beauty, wit, grace, dance, song, and goodness. Essential attributes though these might well have proved for aspiring young women of previous centuries, they will hardly cut the mustard for anyone hoping to survive and thrive throughout the twenty-first. Due to a series of unforeseen developments and plot twists, Sleeping Beauty is *cursed to sleep for a hundred years*. If today's Sleeping Beauty is to be *blessed to live for a hundred years*, she is going to need a very different skill set to help her make the most of this extra time in the face of all the challenges of an evermore unpredictable world. As we celebrate her christening, it strikes me that this is merely one of the very many new starts that this baby will have to manage during her recently embarked-upon life.

Much further along the longevity spectrum, and rapidly approaching the springtime of my senility, I often find myself looking back over a lifetime that has witnessed not only massive societal changes but also many profound, sometimes painful, personal transitions. According to the great British statesman Sir Winston Churchill, success is the ability to move from one failure to another with no loss of enthusiasm.

On the basis of that very generous yardstick, I am comforted to think of my own biblically allotted lifespan as the most tremendous success. Over a period of almost three score years and ten, I have moved from modern linguist and international conference interpreter to writer and broadcaster, to keynote speaker, to parent and homemaker, to building contractor and business development networker, to longevity and well-being research fellow and cross-generational mentor—the list is still a work in progress. Transitions involving the challenges of a new job, the excitement of a new relationship, or the demands for personal growth required by responsibilities such as parenthood or mentorship may prove exhilarating, if occasionally exhausting. Working your way through the various phases of truly transformative transitions is usually a difficult and stressful process. The relief unleashed by sighting that metaphorical light at the end of the tunnel may blot out the pain endured to get there. It is, however, useful to remember what and how you were feeling when eventually the catalyst arrived that propelled you to "start digging."

My own most recent alert came when I was watching a gardening program. The presenter moved from the joyous profusion of colors, shapes, and textures in his herbaceous borders to focus on a sad little specimen lurking disconsolately in a pot by his shed. For the benefit of the camera, he picked it up, the better to display its full wretchedness to the viewers at home. The poor plant seemed embarrassed by this sudden intrusion, and a few of its remaining leaves fluttered lethargically toward the ground. The presenter was undeterred. Yanking the plant from the pot by its spindly stem, he pointed to a knotted tangle of roots circling endlessly round and round and interwoven into an impenetrable, tightly knitted ball. "This is what happens," he observed, "when a healthy plant is neglected and can't find enough sustenance when it's trying to grow. It's now so weak that it can't send out roots to nurture itself from the surrounding environment. *This plant is potbound!*" He paused and stared mournfully into the camera for full dramatic effect. "Unless it's repotted soon, this plant is going to choke itself to death."

I had to restrain myself from cheering out loud: not at the potential fate of this poor plant, but at my own sudden insight of incandescent lucidity. In one short sentence, the presenter had diagnosed the malaise from which I had been suffering. Mr. Gardening Guy had nailed it. This was what was wrong with *me*! For quite some time, I'd been assailed by this nagging feeling that my own increasingly pointless efforts to flourish were going around in circles. The commitments, pleasures, and pastimes that once I had enjoyed no longer seemed to engage or sustain me. Call it existential angst or ennui, or call it simply tired-all-the-time fatigue, but the more I struggled to ignore whatever it was, the worse the symptoms became. It was like fighting against the constraints of a straitjacket. Suddenly, the diagnosis implied was beyond all reasonable doubt. *I was potbound.* I'd been living in an environment that had worked well enough, but now I was feeling stifled by it. Not only was it stunting my growth, it was jeopardizing my well-being. Hence the insistent sense that something was *not quite right*. It was clear that the time had come to extract myself from my current situation and to set out in search of a new, more propitious environment. It was equally clear that no convenient Mr. Gardening Guy was ever going to organize my own repotting for me. However tough it might prove, and however much support I might garner along the way, this was a process of self-renewal that I'd have to work out for myself.

This realization that I needed to "repot" would soon be directing my next steps, the decisions I would make, and what I wanted for my future. What I learned along my journey of repotting—a journey that would take me to a whole new country and an undertaking full of possibility and growth—also offers, I hope, a useful new model for navigating the increasing number of transitions that we are all called upon to make throughout life in the modern world.

And so my gift to my goddaughter, and to anyone embarking on a new stage in life, would be an understanding of how best to master the challenging and often-daunting process of moving on and branching out. My gift would be proficiency in the art of "repotting."

POTBOUND

How do you know when you are potbound?
Is repotting the best solution for you?

First of all, it's important to understand that the potbound predicament is no respecter of age. The very tendrils that you have yourself grown into the soil around you can stifle you at any stage of your life: young, old, middle-aged, retired, at the peak of personal achievement, or at the apogee of a professional career. For many people, the descent into becoming potbound is a perniciously gradual process, a continuous drip-drip accumulation of apparently minor issues. Although the realization of the full extent of potbound damage may come as a sudden shock, rather like the dramatic demise of a majestic oak that no one realized was riddled with rot, it is not the focus of this book to deal with the aftermath of unexpected, cataclysmic events such as those occasioned by life-changing accidents or injuries. Although such tragic reversals may generate similar feelings and require similar solutions, the potbound phenomenon is a malaise that creeps up over time. Often the damage being done is so stealthy and surreptitious that you're unaware of the harm being wrought and fail to spot the

3

well-camouflaged signs until they've made quite serious inroads. You may, for instance, have sought refuge in sticking your head in the sand and successfully managed to ignore the fact that your innate tendency to grow and develop has somehow been arrested. Or perhaps you've never had the time to notice that instead of continuing to flourish and blossom, you've actually started to wilt and wither.

Of course, it's easy to identify that things aren't working when you're dealing with inanimate objects. Even dug in deep beneath the most substantial sand dune, most of us would still recognize when the boiler has exploded, the laptop has crashed, or that we've just dropped our smartphone in a puddle, smashed the screen, and backed over it with the car for good measure. It's far more difficult to establish that there's something seriously amiss when we're considering a lifelong career, an intimate relationship, or some other profoundly personal situation. When we find ourselves confronted with a complex set of circumstances, it's often hard to separate what's important and what's not.

If you struggle to get out of bed to go to work one grim winter's morning, does that immediately mean that you should call it a day and quit your job? If your partner squeezes toothpaste from the middle of the tube, cracks his knuckles while watching television, or consistently taps the top of his boiled egg in that irritating fashion, does that necessarily warrant a call to the divorce lawyer? Maybe. Maybe not. Perhaps none of these seemingly nebulous niggles would be sufficient in themselves to trigger a dramatic change of direction, but they might gradually lead you to a tipping point, or alert you to a more fundamental issue that you haven't yet admitted or identified. It's not the knuckle-cracking or the murderous urges in themselves, but it's the way they add up to a dangerous accumulation of repressed feelings.

Why are we so adept at covering up and ignoring our instincts? Perhaps part of the problem is that we're conditioned to resist the idea that things aren't working. From an early age we're drip-fed the notion that, if we try hard enough, we'll eventually overcome the problems that life throws at us. We live in a society that rightly prizes resilience, grit, and perseverance. Just like previous world-war generations, we're exhorted to pack all our troubles in our old knapsacks and smile, smile, smile. Staying power, the stuff of true champions, is justifiably lauded. In such a competitive environment, no one feels comfortable looking like a quitter who hasn't given 100 percent commitment to the job in hand. None of us wants to fall at the next hurdle, but how do you know when you're beating a dead horse?

Herein lies the rub. If you don't learn how to ask yourself the right kind of questions, you'll never have a hope in hell of coming up with the right kind of answers, and you risk finding yourself climbing to the top of a very impressive ladder only to discover that it's up against the wrong wall. Or that you've plowed a wonderfully straight furrow, but it's in the wrong field. Feel free to dream up a suitably compelling metaphor to cover your own particular situation, but you get the idea: Fail to question your own feelings, motivations, and behaviors, and you're soon on the path to being potbound.

So how do we start framing the kind of questions that might deliver answers best geared to ensure our overall wellness, well-being, and sense of purpose? I believe the right questions involve the heart, as opposed to the head, far more frequently than we imagine. Too often our conscious selves elect to ignore our unconscious wisdom, often at the expense of physical and mental health. Sometimes we may even be aware of this clash between our intellectual and emotional selves, but we make the mistake of brushing aside our gut feelings and pushing on regardless. Far more frequently we simply fail to recognize what our heart is trying to tell us. The writing might be on the wall, but we haven't acquired the emotional literacy to read what the message says. In the absence of some handy key to decipher the Rosetta Stone of our innermost feelings, we could be mired in our potbound predicament forever until we learn to crack our own code.

LOOK FOR PHYSICAL AND BEHAVIORAL CLUES—IN YOURSELF AND ALSO IN OTHERS

It may seem counterintuitive, but, if we are to develop this emotional literacy, it is worth paying attention in the first instance to physical clues. Sometimes the body expresses what the mind represses, so don't discount the possibility that a physical symptom could be a sign of feelings that you are barely aware of. If you feel the urgent need to drink a bottle of wine or polish off a pint of Ben & Jerry's after every phone call with your mother, there are probably more forces at work than those of mere physical cravings. Ask yourself, before you pass out clutching the pinot grigio, facedown in the family-size container of cookie dough, are your own eating, drinking, and sleeping habits pointing to unresolved or maybe even unrecognized problems? Warning signals from skin eruptions to changes in heart rate to tense body language can also serve as powerful indicators that something is amiss. A friend of mine grew so depressed over her distressingly disfiguring skin complaint that she seriously considered giving up the work she loved due to what she assumed was stress. As part of her responsibilities, she was often obliged to deal with a certain British television and radio personality whose well-publicized record on charitable fundraising had resulted in his being honored by a knighthood. Given the

7

star's status and celebrity, my friend found her attempts to avoid being in the same room as him increasingly difficult to justify. It was only after his death, when it transpired that this widely fawned-upon knight of the realm had been operating with impunity for many years as one of Britain's most prolific sex offenders, that she finally realized that this man had been responsible—literally—for bringing her out in a rash.

Apart from observing physical clues, try also drilling down into your habitual patterns. In the crucially restorative area of sleep, for example, most of us will have experienced those long dark nights of the soul spent tossing and turning and wrestling with genuine and recognized worries. Others will have spent endlessly unproductive hours conked out from apparent exhaustion but in reality trying to escape from unresolved issues by resorting to chemical oblivion. From hair loss to high blood pressure to nonspecific back pain—a cursory glance at any agony aunt column provides telling insights into the range of physical symptoms that are often pointing to deeper emotional issues.

Sometimes the clues to your potbound status are behavioral rather than physical, and they can be harder to identify—at least in yourself. Before you try to spot any warning signs in your own behavior, it's helpful to train your eye by watching the behavior of total strangers. I'm not suggesting that you start scrutinizing people with the obsessive attention of some swivel-eyed psychopath, just that you discreetly try spotting the clues. One evening, around the time of my own potbound epiphany, I was sitting in my favorite local Italian restaurant and observed a couple out for dinner together. The moment the man was seated, he smacked his iPhone down on the table. The woman's eyelids flickered. Without missing a beat, she saw his iPhone, raised him a Samsung Galaxy, and threw in a mini iPad. Before long, he was ostentatiously ogling the waitress's legs. She countered by giving the wine waiter's arm an overly familiar pat. I followed this elaborate quadrille of active indifference for over an hour. Neither of them could have spoken more than a dozen words to the other as they parried their way through their respective plates of pasta. From what I could make out, there was neither the energy nor the animus between them to suggest the aftermath of a blazing row. It was simply that these two attractive, ostensibly success-ful people were wholeheartedly engaged in the process of passive-aggressively irritating each other to death.

Perhaps these two strangers were aware of their unhappiness but were too terminally potbound even to be bothered to break up, or perhaps, like so many of us, they had no idea what was actually going on. The point is that the best way to recognize yourself as potbound is to identify the spectrum of potbound symptoms playing out in other people. Many of you will have consulted the burned-out physician too exhausted to diagnose a decapitation. He's scribbled out your prescription on his pad before you've even finished describing your symptoms. Or perhaps you've come across the poor end-of-her-tether mother so frazzled that she forgets to pick up her kids from school and is constantly trying to microwave oven-ready meals in the top rack of her dishwasher. She's so overloaded with other people's wants and needs that she has nothing but debilitating disregard for herself. Or perhaps you have worked with one of those complacent or bully-boy bosses who stubbornly refuse to stand aside, so smugly self-satisfied with their long-gone successes that they are unable to see the threat of competitive disruption that's about to destroy their organizations. Witness the slew of failed Pol Potbounds in the retail business!

Once you start looking for examples of potbound behavior and analyzing the symptoms, you'll gradually become more and more proficient at identifying them in yourself. Perhaps you begin to recognize those constant sighs of world-weary exhaustion as signs of about-to-blow frustration? You ask yourself why it is that you're always snapping at the kids. Maybe you begin to realize that you're forever watching the clock at work, or that you're constantly swearing at inanimate objects and arguing with the radio. Perhaps you question whether your ostensible diligence in working on weekends is in reality a way of avoiding your partner. And was it really just an accident this morning when you reached out and whacked him on the nose instead of hitting the snooze button? You may find yourself defaulting to knee-jerk negativity and grumpy responses, or you may realize that you're simply trundling along, somehow managing to survive another godawful day without the life-enhancing seasoning of the merest dash of *joie de vivre*.

Despite the tsunami of smartwatches, apps, and Fitbits widely available nowadays, there still don't seem to be any high-tech solutions on offer designed to track the most important things in life. As far as I can see, there's no app around that tells you that you're behaving like a jerk, that you shouldn't be so thin-skinned, or that you really ought to try and lighten up a little. So how can you increase awareness of your own behaviors? How can you detect any potentially potbound signals? When you're dealing with deeply personal issues, it seems that only low-tech solutions will do. I've always found that keeping a diary, quite apart from fitting Oscar Wilde's bill of ensuring that there's always something sensational to read on the train, also provides a rich seam to mine, unearth, and identify cause-and-effect patterns.

If you can find the time to keep a daily journal, however perfunctory, you'll start to recognize recurrent themes and learn how to identify when and why they happen. Imagine, for example, that you've been called out for snapping at your work colleagues. You didn't even realize that you were being touchy, but when you look back over your journal, you notice that every time you embark on an undertaking that interests you, you're somehow dragooned into dealing with other colleagues' pressing issues and end up doing a suboptimal job on your own pet project. Suddenly you understand not only why you're irritated at work but also why, when you return home to find your children's sneakers scattered untidily in the hall, you explode with an outburst out of all proportion to the misalignment of a few random Nikes.

For me, a journal provides a cathartic lightning rod for channeling all manner of inchoate feelings. It's a useful structure for identifying patterns and explaining my otherwise often inexplicably bad behavior. And it's also a secure repository for offloading the arrant drivel that's constantly swirling around in my head. Many people I know learn how to interpret their emotions and the patterns at play in their lives by paying attention to their decisions, behaviors, and reactions in all sorts of different situations. If you only ever eat pizza, or play the same old music, or still wear that purple eyeshadow some cruel clown suggested was hip way back in the 1960s, you might want to ask yourself whether these are actively satisfying decisions or whether your developmental clock has simply stopped. Even the amount of pleasure you now derive from the hobbies and pastimes that you once enthusiastically engaged in—whether your interest lay in art, music, crafts, cooking, travel, exercise, or sports—may alert you to when you're in, or when you're close to falling into, potbound territory.

EXAMINE YOUR PAST

Another way to diagnose ourselves as potbound is to look at times in our past when we have been unhappy—and to attempt a retrospective diagnosis. This can be especially useful as a way of identifying our own particular triggers and warning signals. When I look back over my own life, for example, I can now see all sorts of telltale signs that I didn't recognize at the time—particularly from the point at which I entered the world of work. Although my childhood and adolescence could hardly be described as a remorselessly merry experience, I found that school and university at least provided roadmaps that were clear and easy to follow. They provided stages, scores, and targets that were reassuringly simple to understand, if often challenging to achieve. Like many children of my generation, I was given to believe that how my life panned out would be down to intelligence or effort—ideally and most successfully by a combination of both. On this basis, I understood what I was supposed to be doing and generally felt that I was making progress if I managed to do it. The expectations and goals of the education system were equally simple to comprehend: Do the work, pass the exams, party as hard as you can with any residual time available. Wash—Rinse—Repeat Cycle.

Work, however, was an infinitely more complex ball game. Not only did metrics for meaningful development in the workplace seem more difficult to track, but the right track itself was not always easy to identify. After I graduated with a degree in modern languages, my first job was as an international conference interpreter. The task of a simultaneous interpretation is both physically and mentally taxing: You're called on to function as a multilingual peacekeeping force conciliating a war of words being constantly waged in your head. The process involves tuning in to someone speaking in one language, assimilating their content, tone, and nuances, and then converting the entire meaning and message almost instantly into another language. Get it wrong, and all hell breaks loose! For me, gaining proficiency in the profession involved a steep learning curve, and most of the time my brain ached, but from the outset, I loved the work, its challenges, and the vibrant community and camaraderie associated with it. Over a period of fifteen years, I was working all over the world for many major international organizations, including the European Union, the United Nations, and the world's leading heads of state and government at their annual World Economic Summits.

There came a time, however, when I could feel my enthusiasm waning. International travel, once a perk of the job, deteriorated into a grind. Days spent listening to the deliberately dishonest drivel of the self-appointed great and good, once rich raw material for post-conference banter in the bar, became insufferable. One day, in the middle of a major environmental conference, I suddenly found that I couldn't bear to hear one more minute of virtue-signaling politicians and their pious posturing. It's bad news for any interpreter who no longer wants even to listen, let alone interpret. For the first time in my life, I felt I was going around in circles or—worse—going through the motions in an increasingly depressing downward spiral. At the time, I couldn't quite put my finger on what was wrong. What I did know, however, was that something had to change.

LOOK FOR TELLTALE PATTERNS

Deeply personal potbound predicaments are often difficult and distressing to dissect. Although they may be precipitated by external events, the emotions and reactions involved are usually rooted in patterns that you might well have spent a lifetime reenacting while notably failing to recognize. Since these patterns are automatic, compulsive, and emotionally charged, they can make you revert to bad habits without consciously understanding the reasons behind them or the feelings caught up within them. Some of these patterns might stem from your childhood. They link back to the way you were treated as a child and the way you felt and reacted way back then when you were small, vulnerable, and powerless. Once you learn how to recognize and trace these patterns, you can set about learning how to check and, if necessary, abort your instinctive reactions.

In France, the land of rationalism and reasoning, you wouldn't get far by invoking your tragic tale of failed potty training as an excuse for blowing up the Louvre. "*Il faut s'assumer!*" the French gendarmes would remonstrate angrily as they carted you off for a jolly good grilling, probably in the imperfect subjunctive. From early childhood, French children are encouraged to "*s'assumer*"—to take responsibility for their actions: in other words, to Grow Up! My Anglo-Saxon brethren, by contrast, show far less inclination to take the rap for our own behavior and will happily play the "blame the parents/upbringing" card at every opportunity. Like Philip Larkin, that most gloriously gloomy of British poets, Anglo-Saxons have always argued, with a typically Anglo-Saxon directness of language and the employment of a four-letter expletive much in evidence in English football stadiums, that your mom and dad have done an extremely good job at screwing you up. Although hardly a ringing endorsement of your own or your parents' parenting efforts, Larkin makes the generous concession that the generally suboptimal outcome is no one individual parent's fault. Since patterns are handed down from generation unto generation, so the logic goes, neither you, nor I, nor anyone can avoid ending up controlled by patterns that leave us all, to a very large extent, quite well and truly messed up.

Give me the child until he is seven, claimed Aristotle, and I will show you the man. It's alarming to concede that, at so young an age, you've already been molded into your abiding moral and emotional shape. Certainly, up until the age of puberty, you will almost certainly—if unconsciously—adopt the positive and negative behaviors, belief systems, moods, attitudes, and insecurities of your primary caregivers. Within your immediate family environment, you'll then continue to absorb how to be and how to behave with others, how to engage with the world, and how to relate to yourself. Exposure to negative behaviors obviously increases your chances of adopting them. It's been said that you are the average of the five people you spend the most time with, and medical research consistently shows that if you live, or even hang out, with drinkers, smokers, or people who are obese, your chances of drinking, smoking, and overeating are massively increased. Abusive parents create children who are often hurtful and abusive toward themselves and others. In time, many children adopt the selfsame destructive patterns as their parents, and thus the cycle of baked-in bad behavior continues ad infinitum.

Not all patterns are necessarily bad per se. You probably know lots of individuals whose behaviors are eminently socially acceptable but who are also operating unthinkingly in line with their inherited patterns. The classic people-pleaser, the tireless do-gooder, the irrepressible life-and-soul-of the-party funster: These stalwarts of the social and community scene are equally caught up in their own compulsive patterns that control the way they function. You may well find that your own patterns are difficult to isolate because, over time, those behaviors have become so regular and consistent that you've come to believe that your patterns are actually the authentic *you*. So how can we learn to break out of the circle? How can we exercise the element of personal choice in naming, taming, and reframing our patterns? An entente cordiale that melds French and Anglo-Saxon attitudes might constitute a helpful approach. Perhaps the French insistence on growing up merged with the Anglo-Saxon emphasis on looking back might help us all move forward?

TRACE THE PATTERNS BACK

Psychoanalysis falls well beyond the scope of this book, but often a few simple sessions of self-interrogation will yield potentially transformational insights. Spend some time looking back over your own upbringing. Try thinking about the various influences brought to bear on you in your early years and how they may be impacting areas of your adult life right now. And remain alert to the fact that your own behavior may not simply be a matter of copycat adoption; it could also be a reaction or rebellion that you've come up with in order to differentiate or distance yourself from a parent. Ask yourself:

1. How were you treated physically and emotionally by your parents or caregivers? Were they, for example, undemonstrative, unreliable, cold, sarcastic, depressed, moody, dismissive? If so, have you assimilated any of these traits? Or have you reacted by moving to the other end of the happy–demonstrative spectrum and ended up a Pollyanna–Pavarotti love child?

2. On what basis did you feel valued? As a child, did you feel that you were being constantly judged, criticized, or subjected to impossibly high expectations? Were your parents prejudiced or patronizing? Dogmatic or intolerant? Inflexible or hypocritical? Are you mirroring any of these behaviors? Or have you been so coddled, reinforced, and pampered that you've developed into an insufferably self-entitled jerk?

3. Were your parents subject to compulsive behaviors or addictions? We're not talking only about obvious addictions such as drugs, gambling, and alcohol, but also excessive behavior in areas such as shopping, tidying, working, exercise, religious practice, or hypochondria. Do you replicate these or any similarly compulsive patterns? Or perhaps you reacted against your parents' grotesque materialism by denouncing all worldly goods and retreating to a life of quiet contemplation in an ashram in Maharashtra?

4. What about your own self-image? To what extent is that associated with your parents and/or upbringing? Were your role models, for instance, narcissistic, selfish, jealous, elitist, or desperate to be admired? Do you recognize yourself in any of these categories? Or have you cut loose, changed your name in court, and attempted

to forge your own character without apparent reference to anything but your own internal compass?

5. What's your attitude toward money and work? Are you a spendthrift or a miser? Are you consistently up to your neck in debt? Do you feel trapped in a job that you find meaningless? Are you constantly overcommitted, stressed, and in danger of burning out? Again, what attitudes observed in your parents/caregivers do you now see playing out in yourself? Are you replicating or rejecting their behaviors?

6. In terms of self-confidence: Were you made to feel that, whatever you did, you were never good enough? Were the adults around you fearful and anxious or, in contrast, in constant denial about pressing problems? Were they dominating or controlling?

7. What about sex and relationships? Were you brought up thinking that "sex" was a dirty word? Or that rampant promiscuity was par for the course? Or that more or less any sexual activity was perfectly acceptable so long as it didn't frighten the horses?

8. What boundaries, if any, were you given? Did your parents consistently transgress healthy physical, mental, or emotional barriers? Did they invade your privacy?

Did they try to force-feed you with their own beliefs? Did they attempt to control you with physical or mental fear? Or did they constantly belittle you and disregard your feelings?

This isn't an exercise in blaming anyone. It's an effort to recognize why you feel and behave the way that you do. Only then can you learn consciously and intentionally to *respond* to any given situation or stimulus as opposed to *reacting* automatically. By taking control of your emotions in this way, you can start to trust them, and this will help you figure out how it is that those tendrils of yours have gradually started binding and imprisoning you rather than nourishing and enriching you.

NAME IT AND TAME IT

Recognizing, understanding, and interpreting your emotions is a crucial step toward diagnosing yourself as potbound. But it also allows you to examine your actual situation with a clear head and spell out what the problems really are. The key is to try to be as specific as possible. As a doctor operating in a deprived area of the northwest of England during the immediate aftermath of World War II, my father had his fair share of challenges, but the issue he found impossible to deal with was when patients were unable to explain clearly what was wrong with them—something he came to call the Dreaded Definition Deficiency.

Bad cases of DDD used to test my father's patience to the limit. A patient would present in his consulting room, usually at the end of excessively long office hours, slump down wearily on a chair, and gaze hopelessly into the middle distance. "I don't know what it is, doctor," the poor patient would invariably complain, "but it's doing my bloody head in!" The symptom "doing my bloody head in" featured nowhere in his *British Medical Journal* literature, and it was therefore down to my father's powers of divination as much as his diagnostic skills to identify the mysterious malady. Describe the problem accurately, my father would say, and you're already halfway to finding the cure. The same holds true for those of us who end up suspecting that we are potbound. As far as possible, and with total honesty, it's important to identify correctly why it is that we're feeling lost, stuck, or forever going around in circles. Because sometimes we don't need to go to the radical lengths of repotting our entire lives; we just need to understand a certain behavior and change it.

Words are the most powerful resource that mankind has ever invented. *Sticks and stones may break my bones, but words will never hurt me.* Of all the nonsensical nursery jingles, this one always struck me as one of the silliest. In my experience, words are invested with an infinite capacity to hurt or to heal, to inspire or discourage, to soothe or incense. As an international conference interpreter, I regularly witnessed complex negotiations on the brink of success suddenly falter and fail over one ill-judged throwaway comment. On the other hand, I have also observed long-standing feuds instantly resolved by a few kind words. Disputes between entire nations can escalate wildly on the basis of often trivial misunderstandings, and, equally, violent disagreements can be put to rest with honest expressions of contrition and words of forgiveness.

In much the same way, and in a vast number of personal situations that are apparently "stuck," finding the right words can provide a crucial catalyst for breaking the deadlock. When we are feeling potbound, we need to recognize that we are in a vulnerable state and seek to become our own negotiator, calming ourselves down, helping ourselves to think straight, and thereby finding a way out.

Let's say you are feeling fed up because you believe your professional career is going nowhere. Acknowledge the feeling by all means, but take a step back and ask yourself one simple question: "Is this belief true?" Is it an incontrovertible fact that you are really going nowhere, or do you feel like a failure simply because you missed out on a particular promotion? Then, keep going with the "Is it true?" routine.

Is it true that you're genuinely a failure for missing out on the promotion, or is your boss a clueless incompetent incapable of recognizing the best candidate for the job? Or were you, in fact, an excellent candidate who simply happened to lose out to someone who has more experience and can add demonstrably more value to the business?

You get the idea. Just keep asking the "Is it true?" question until you drill down to the last, tiny, remaining nugget of what is incontrovertibly true. By the time you arrive at this stage, you'll probably find that instead of being overwhelmed by the apocalyptic "I'm a failure and my career is a disaster," the plain truth is infinitely less dramatic and presents you with a far more acceptable picture. Perhaps the essential truth is nothing more painful than that you need to take a course and improve, for example, the IT, coding, or marketing skills that will put you more clearly in the frame for future promotion. You've successfully reduced your catastrophic career to a minor gap in your skill set.

RECOGNIZE YOUR OWN
POWER TO CONTROL

Once you have dialed down the emotional heat by identifying and giving a specific name to the underlying problem, the next step is to categorize it. Is it an external issue or an internal issue? If it's external, how much control, if any, do you have over it? And if it's internal, what can you realistically do to overcome it? Some external issues—the loss of a loved one or a serious disease, for example—are so extreme that, however hard you try, they cannot be sorted out. I call them "black-hole problems." Nothing that you or anyone else can do can change the unassailable reality of a bereavement, the onset of an incurable illness, or the fact that someone no longer loves you. In such situations, there are no solutions to make the problem go away; all you can do is try to adjust to the situation. To resist is to indulge in the pointless and damaging exercise of "black-hole behavior."

In the mid-1980s, when I first embarked on a career in writing, many British newspapers were regularly disrupted by labor strikes. Luckily for the world's press barons, however, the old labor-intensive printing methods were on the way out. The advent of modern computer facilities enabled journalists to input copy directly, thus completely bypassing the troublesome high priests of the print unions. In a classic case of black-hole behavior, union leaders refused to see the digital writing on the wall and remained stubbornly stuck in their fixed hot-metal mindsets and insistence on labor strikes. Their resistance was futile. Almost overnight, the skills that once held press barons hostage became irrelevant and any attempt to counter that immutable reality was simply to howl at the moon.

However bitter a pill it is to swallow, in the face of black-hole problems, the only rational response is acceptance. Sadly, you're never going to be invited to sing *Tosca* at La Scala if you sound like a hyena with a strangulated hernia. Nor is there much likelihood of your making it to prima ballerina with the Bolshoi if you dance like a woman with an inner ear infection. Realism should dictate acceptance, however reluctant, of the fact that you're never going to take the stage by storm. This does not mean, however, that you cannot learn how to respond effectively to any given black-hole problem.

REFRAME THE PROBLEM

You might not be able to tame a black-hole problem, but you can reframe it—by recognizing, for example, that your lack of talent for the performing arts should not necessarily negate your enthusiasm. You might discover a talent for directing, costume, lighting, or makeup, or you might even harness your private passion for Excel spreadsheets to catapult yourself into a career as a theatrical impresario. Alternatively, you might elect to pursue a completely unrelated area of endeavor in which you truly shine and use your spare time and money to enjoy watching other professionals, more conventionally talented than yourself in the performing arts, as they strut their stuff onstage. Whatever your decision, in the face of a black-hole problem, acceptance is the first step on the road to progress.

Events such as the Paralympics and the Invictus Games have gifted the world many inspirational examples of individuals who have responded magnificently to their own black-hole problems. With grit, imagination, and resilience, competitors consistently demonstrate how they have successfully reframed their physical disabilities into a celebration of outstanding achievement. Few people in civilian life will ever be exposed to the extreme degrees of sudden shock, loss, and trauma that the heroic individuals of the Invictus Games have endured, but their lessons in reframing ostensibly insuperable reversals hold true for everyone.

If you are in a professional rut and are wise enough to have a go at the "Is it true?" exercise, you might discover that your potbound symptoms have been caused by the fact that it is your employer that is the black-hole problem. In the majority of international institutions for which I've worked, many genuine highfliers become understandably frustrated when their deserved ascent to the very top of the organizational ladder is blocked by office politics. It's tough for the stellar Swede to find himself overlooked in favor of the low-grade lush from Luxembourg.

In such unfair working environments where it's a matter of who you know or where you were born rather than what you know or can do, it's tempting to allow yourself to become dragged into a downward spiral of potbound victimhood. Who wouldn't feel aggrieved when their stratospheric superiority is being so blatantly and cynically sidelined? And yet, despite the egregious unfairness of the situation, you are not a helpless victim. Like the wounded individual deciding to train for the Invictus Games, you still have the power to choose your response. Back in civilian life, you might elect to fight to change the corporate culture. You might decide to quit. Or you might reassess the problem and decide to stick around for a pension guaranteed by the kind of institution that coughs up the cash irrespective of whether you're world-class or truly woeful. No one is judging you. As long as you make an intentional and reasoned decision, then you've actively elected how to move on in your own way. You've successfully reframed your ostensible reversal and avoided falling into the big, black hole of professional victimhood.

Sometimes, of course, we like to think that a situation is beyond our control when it isn't. In less irretrievably Bob's Your Uncle/Jobs for the Boys environments, the professionally potbound predicament is frequently due to an

intertwined combination of internal and external constraints—an amalgam that we might usefully term a "hybrid
problem." It may well be true that external forces such as
dependents or family commitments make it very difficult for
you to travel, to relocate, to undertake the necessary professional development, or to assume the additional professional
risks and responsibilities required for promotion. If you're
being totally honest with yourself, however, you might admit
too that your decision not to take a chance and throw your
hat in the ring is also due to your own internal reluctance to
change or to challenge yourself or to grow.

At other times, a situation may be entirely internally
driven. A friend of mine was forever telling us how "useless" she was at anything "involving numbers" and therefore
"totally hopeless" at sorting out her finances. This same friend
is also eminently capable of catering effortlessly for large
events, producing exquisite meals of which a Michelin-starred
chef would be justifiably proud, and training teams of
silver-service staff to wait on even the most discerning
of clients. To her many good friends, it seemed completely
incomprehensible that such an outstandingly competent
woman should find any trouble whatsoever in getting her
head around basic budgeting. As we prodded her with a few
gentle questions, it transpired that her father never had the
patience to help her when she was struggling with her math

homework (although, apparently, he always seemed to find time to help her brother). Furthermore, he had impressed on her that, "because she was clearly not academic," a proficiency in cooking was "the best way for a girl like you to land a good husband—just like your mother did!"

Stifling our outrage, we encouraged our friend to consign these half-baked notions to the trash can of demented daddy-drivel where they clearly belonged and set about introducing her to a few simple financial planning apps available on her smartphone. It turned out that she was a natural. Within a week, she had signed up for an online bookkeeping course and within a year had doubled the profits of her burgeoning catering business. In other words, she had successfully managed to name, tame, and reframe the problem underlying her situation in an exercise along the following lines:

1. Name the problem: I'm bad at math.

2. Tame the problem: Someone in my life once told me that I was bad at math. Because that person and his views were of crucial importance to me at that time, I believed this assessment of me to be incontrovertibly true. I now realize that this judgment may not have been correct after all.

3. Reframe the problem: I was once given the notion that I was bad at math. Thanks to the technological support around nowadays, I realize that I'm actually very good at working with numbers and more than capable of running an extremely successful business.

You may find a similar "Name—Tame—Reframe" technique helpful when you're trying to distance yourself from negative belief patterns. With practice, "I *am* a failure" can be made to morph into the less emotionally charged "I *feel like* a failure" and end up being completely watered down into the far more manageable "I've had a thought about feeling like a failure and now I choose to let go of that thought." In time, you might even succeed in emulating the mindset of Thomas Edison, King of Reframers and inventor of the electric light bulb. He chose to reframe his multiple flops not as failures, but as ten thousand highly instructive examples of inventions that didn't work—innovations that kept moving him ever closer to the goal he'd set out to achieve.

Whatever the material facts of your own situation, and however you elect to reframe them, you can always create an internal narrative that makes sense to you and helps you to move on. You may not be able to control the facts of your story, but with the help of the right words, you can always control the *genre*. Still recovering from an excoriating divorce, a friend of mine recently took her engagement ring to a jewelry designer to have it reset as a pendant. For her, this symbolic gesture represented closure, and she sobbed over the ultimate demise of her marriage all the way to the workshop. "Welcome to the Lemonade Club," said the designer, as soon as she showed him the engagement ring. She shot him a quizzical look. "Turning lemons into lemonade," he responded, picking up the ring for closer inspection. "You're my fifth divorcée this week!" My friend's whole take on her deeply distressing personal situation was instantly reframed, and she ended up laughing all the way home. The tragic tale of duplicity, deceit, and disillusion that had threatened to drag her down into potbound depression had been magically reframed into an amusing story with her ex as the butt of the joke.

CHOOSE TO REPOT

So, let's say you've found yourself feeling potbound, you've taken the time to consider whether those feelings are a true reflection of your situation, and you've examined the situation clearly enough to know that it is not a black-hole problem and that it's something that can be changed. That's when you can rest assured that the process of repotting will help. Terrific! You're making great progress, but as we all know, it's one thing to recognize a problem; it's quite another to do something about it.

I recently read a headline that stated that 47.2 is the age of deepest desolation—an assertion that made me unconscionably happy, as it's encouraging to learn that you're already well past your misery peak. Although the potbound predicament can kick in at any stage of life, the classic midlife crisis has attracted the most attention for obvious reasons. By the time you reach deep middle age, it's particularly disconcerting to accept that much of the training and many of the assumptions, beliefs, and behaviors that have worked well for you thus far may now be totally unfit for purpose. You might well find it difficult to recognize, at this advanced stage of your life, that what got you here won't get you there. Instead, you may decide to cling desperately to the receding wreckage of your previous status or to your position as a PIP (Previously Important Person) instead of actively repotting for the next stage.

I understand only too well how terrifying a challenge it is to start reframing the experiences from the complex hinterland of your previous life before setting off, in the springtime of your senility, to discover who you might yet become. How infinitely more comfortable you'd feel just slipping back into your old, well-worn patterns even though they may no longer challenge you, enthuse you, or even work for you. If, like me, you'll never again see sixty, it's increasingly likely that your "hybrid problem" may be rooted in that fact that extended life expectancy has left you at a loose end in your elongated life. You feel full of hard-earned experience and wisdom and are still enthusiastic to contribute, but you're stymied by the lack of opportunities, culture, or institutions designed to help you make the most of your extra gifted years. You feel frustrated at being shunted up the sidings of life when there's still plenty of juice left in the tank.

I can vividly remember the second point at which I faced up to my own potbound feelings and realized that it was time for another change. My post-interpreting career in writing had led to radio and television work, and this in turn had led to a series of lucrative speaking engagements. As with interpreting, I grew to love the professional speaking business with a passion. Assimilating often-complex briefs; distilling the most important messages; learning how best to engage an audience—some of these were key skills that I'd already learned as an interpreter, and the others I'd worked hard on trying to perfect. Looking back, though, I can see the same gradual decline in enthusiasm—the same dwindling of motivation. Crunch time came one evening when I was hosting an awards ceremony for the pharmaceutical industry. The event was a full house with over a thousand mainly male be-dinner-jacketed attendees crammed into round tables for dinner in the ballroom of one of London's most celebrated Park Lane hotels. As often happens with these events, there were far too many award categories, and the speeches and photographs were taking far more time than anticipated. By the time we came to the final award, most people had drunk so much they were legless, and the room was growing rowdy. At last, pulling the card from its golden envelope, I came to reading out the winner's name: "And the award for best marketing campaign of the year goes to . . . Germoloids for Hemorrhoids."

The next morning I found myself head-down under my duvet, endlessly replaying the scenes that had followed my announcement as grown men leapt to their feet, wept openly, and punched the air in jubilation. In fact, I was still contemplating this apogee of my glorious career when my agent rang and offered me a generous contract to speak at an event in Monaco. I turned it down flat. It doesn't take a psychotherapist to realize that there's something seriously wrong with you when you just can't be bothered to deliver your own motivational speech. And it's curious how one minor off-key note can herald a major wake-up call. It was as if I'd been living on resources to which I no longer had access and was suddenly waking up to discover that I was wildly overdrawn at the physical and emotional bank. Mentally, I was mortgaged right up to the hilt. A spiritual bandage would no longer work. Nothing less than transformational change would do. At last I was forced to understand that what I needed was what I would now refer to as a radical repotting.

I was terrified because, at last and despite myself, I had been forced to recognize the imperative for serious change. It was now time for me to try and define what that change would be.

SUMMARY

1. Learn to recognize the symptoms of being potbound. Look for clues in your physical health. Identify telltale behavioral signs in others and then turn the spotlight on yourself. Ask yourself how you are feeling. Consider whether you have ever felt potbound in the past and see if you can pinpoint your specific personal symptoms from your own history.

2. Establish the range of reasons responsible for your symptoms. Are you feeling this way because you are stuck in a pattern of unresolved emotions and behaviors? Trace the roots of your dominant patterns and recognize their negative influence.

3. Use the "Is it true?" technique to set emotion to one side, name the problem you face, and thereby give yourself a chance of taming it.

4. Consider the nature of the problem you're facing. Is it something you can control? If you cannot control it, can you reframe the problem in a more constructive way? If you can control it, then ask yourself whether you are ready to try.

5. If the answer is yes, and you are, it's time to start making plans.

POTS AND
PLANS

How do you identify possible repotting
goals that align with who you are,
what makes you feel fulfilled or happy,
and what matters most to you? And
how do you prioritize these goals and
decide which ones to aim for?

The French writer, theologian, mathematician, physicist, inventor, and all-around goddamn genius Blaise Pascal famously observed, "All of humanity's problems stem from man's inability to sit quietly in a room alone." The hyperconnected among you might well argue that if good old Blaise managed to do everything he did while immured alone in his room way back in the seventeenth century, what marvels might he have achieved with all the advantages of twenty-first-century technology? I would argue the complete opposite. Without all the time that he had at his disposal to sit in solitude and think, Pascal would never have managed to achieve half as much as he did.

Many people today are being constantly hijacked by the cacophonous calls on their time and attention. Barely a moment goes by when you're not being manipulated into buying, emoting, engaging, reacting, retweeting, heart-ing, or smiley-face-ing in response to a stream of external stimuli. Even at the best of times, when we're feeling on top of the world, we forget to take time to stop and savor the moment, preferring instead to default to the unthinking reaction or mindlessly succumb to the lure of the next in an endless series of distractions. The point at which you realize you may need to repot rarely comes at the best of times, but this insight could be the prelude to a much brighter future if you can find some mental space to think and plan and dream. If you can carve out periods of peace and quiet to allow yourself to think calmly and objectively, you'll stand a much better chance of doing the groundwork necessary for a successful, well-planned, well-executed, and well-chosen repotting. A wise old garden designer once told me that you achieve better results by putting a $1 plant in a $10 hole than by putting a $10 plant in a $1 hole. (Certainly, that suggestion would seem to tally with the subliminal marketing message promulgated by many of the most expensive private schools!) In other words, if you invest time and energy in doing relevant, preparatory groundwork, any further effort you make will stand a far greater chance of paying dividends.

ASSESS YOUR PLOT

You don't have to be religious or a recovering alcoholic to recognize the words and the wisdom of the "Serenity Prayer":

> God, grant me the serenity to accept the things I
>   cannot change,
> Courage to change the things I can,
> And wisdom to know the difference.

Written by American theologian Reinhold Niebuhr during the Great Depression of the 1930s, this frequently referenced invocation distills the fundamental lesson that you need to learn to become a successful repotter: It's about recognizing the difference between what you can and what you simply cannot change. And just as a good garden designer will always assess a plot before undertaking any new planting, you need to start by taking careful stock of your life as it is right now.

One way to do this is to think of yourself as your own personal brand. Even nomads wandering in the Gobi Desert recognize such top global brands as Facebook, Apple, Google, and Amazon. These behemoths of business spend fortunes enhancing and fine-tuning the potent amalgam of effables, ineffables, tangibles, and intangibles that, taken together, create recognition and value for their respective corporations. Whether you actively strive to create one or not, you also possess a personal brand that encapsulates the essence of who you are and the values you represent. It is more than just a résumé trumpeting your qualifications and accomplishments; it is your core package of portable human skills, the requisite specialist skills that you've managed to assimilate, and also the good reputation that you've conscientiously created over time.

Forward-looking and enlightened human resources professionals are beginning to realize that paper-based qualifications and assessments based on the traditional linear record of institutions attended, qualifications gained, and salaried positions held will not necessarily deliver the best candidate. Most approximately qualified people can be "skilled up" to the requisite standards of a specific job, but no training program can transform a fundamentally toxic character into a modern-day Mother Teresa or turn a congenital shyster into a shining beacon of ethical light. Just as there are no apps to track obnoxious, unacceptable, or narcissistic behavior, there are no formal institutions handing out certificates for valuable professional assets such as ethics, fairness, reliability, honesty, integrity, and flexibility. Even in today's relatively enlightened environment, many individuals in the workplace feel awkward when called on to explain any gaps in the chronological listings of the conventional résumé. Classically, this issue has disproportionately affected women who have taken career breaks to have children or to care for sick or elderly relatives. The effects of the gig economy, however, have catapulted far more people into the same gap-riddled-résumé situation. Future work models requiring increasingly frequent oscillations between paid work and professional or personal development will further add to the swelling numbers in this cohort. A personal brand that demonstrates the skills, characteristics, values, and potential that you represent (as opposed to a blow-by-blow account of every move you've ever made in your personal and professional life) will become an increasingly valuable asset for any repotter. This is particularly true for any individual who's been laid off, taken a career break, or finds themselves at a crossroads wondering which direction to take. It's easy to feel underqualified and, as a consequence, lacking in self-confidence if you're missing out on the validation of an uninterrupted career in a conventional workplace. You may well have been engaged in performing equally valid or demanding activities other than paid employment, but you can't help feeling that your own list of expertise and experience may look a trifle homespun or hand-knitted compared with others who've opted for a more recognized and conventionally rewarded career path. If you can learn how to present your intangible qualities as concrete assets and cite examples of equivalent competences gained in other, possibly unpaid, areas of endeavor, then you can enhance the value of your own personal brand and ease your repotting transition.

So how do you go about achieving this—not solely for the benefit of external agencies but, more importantly, to bolster your own feelings of self-worth and validation? Many years ago, I interviewed a genuinely charismatic woman, the Lord Mayor of Brisbane, the capital city of Queensland, Australia. When Sallyanne Atkinson first arrived in her post, the state of Queensland was universally acknowledged as the last bastion of dyed-in-the-wool Aussie male chauvinism. She had shot to fame during her city's bid to host the 1992 Olympics and, in the process, forged a name for herself as an exceedingly rare phenomenon in those benighted days: a woman of charm and with a lively sense of humor who could cut the political mustard in a heavily, indeed, almost totally male-dominated environment. This novel amalgam soon began to work wonders. Not only did Sallyanne kick-start an entire regeneration program within the city itself, but she was also instrumental in repositioning the hitherto deeply conservative Queensland as a great place for the international community to do business. During the interview, I

asked Sallyanne how she had managed to effect such transformational change in a state laughingly dismissed by fellow
Aussies as a backwater full of "banana-benders." (Don't ask
for a fuller explanation of this Aussie slang expression but,
take it from me, it's not a compliment!) It seems to me that
her answer is as relevant today to any individual repotter as
it was to the Sleazy State successfully repotting itself as the
Sunshine State over thirty years ago. Sallyanne had continued working professionally while bringing up five children
and supporting her partner in his demanding career as a
neurosurgeon, but the insights she shared on transference
of skills still hold true for us all. "I only came into politics
after I had raised a family and looked after a husband," she
told me. "When you've spent a few years with a baby in one
arm, a toddler hanging on your skirt, trying to stir the peas,
stuff the chicken, open the door, and answer the phone, you
have an excellent grounding in trying to deal with twenty
people and a hundred problems all at once!"

Sallyanne's can-do reframe is a helpful place to start
when you're trying to move from who and where you currently are to who and what you're capable of being and
doing. Establish what excites and motivates you—and be
honest about what doesn't! There's no shame in admitting if
those debilitating years of sleepless nights and crying babies
didn't exactly float your boat. Or that the daily grind of

office life and ghastly commute came close to driving you around the bend. From your own richly textured tapestry of responsibilities, challenges, and problem-solving, start teasing out your strengths and weaknesses and identify what your transferable and hitherto-unsung skills might be. A few questions along the following lines might help you compile a more rounded and instructive picture of who you are and what you're capable of doing next:

1. What do you love doing so much that you'd still do it even if you weren't obliged to, weren't expected to, and/or weren't being paid to do it? It could be anything from basket-weaving to brain surgery; pastry-making to plasma physics; rag-rolling to rocket science.

2. Which of the things that you love doing or that interest/ engage you have a practical application or could be of help or interest to others apart from yourself? You may, for instance, love reading for pleasure and wonder what possible practical application that might have. Might you consider channeling this erstwhile solitary activity into volunteering for a local literacy program?

3. Which skills, attributes, or character traits have you developed in pursuing your responsibilities, interests, and projects? Once you start thinking about your role as

a homemaker, for instance, you may start to appreciate your own expertise in areas as varied as logistics, supply management, and conflict resolution as well as acting as chief cook and bottle-washer. Then ask yourself if any of these talents and qualities would be transferable to your next repotted phase. What gaps in your skill set might you need to address in order to make further progress?

4. What have you done that at first sight may seem unremarkable but, on closer inspection, actually demonstrates genuinely valuable and transferable qualities? For instance, an ability to remain cool under pressure, a capacity to prioritize, a talent for building trust, and a genius for getting people to work together.

By way of example, here are the edited highlights of the thought process I scribbled down before embarking on my most recent repotting.

What do I really love?
I love interacting with new people from different countries, languages, and cultures. (Whatever happens, I mustn't ever allow deep middle age—when a

broad mind and a narrow waist swap attributes—to stop me from doing that!)

OK, *but apart from traveling for pleasure, what practical application does that particular set of interests have now I'm no longer working as an interpreter?*

I'm always hearing and reading about businesses, projects, and initiatives that fail miserably because so many people still believe that everyone else should think and operate just like them. We live in a global environment. Surely, and more than ever, cross-cultural communication should be the name of the game? Could I leverage my skill set to help promote such an environment? How? Where? Are there any obvious silos of people around me who could usefully be interacting better with each other? Given increased life expectancy, what about the challenges raised by more and very different generations trying to live and work together?

Which of my skills are transferable and which gaps do I need to address?

On the plus side, I'm used to being "self-unemployed" and operating as an independent self-starter. I'm happy dealing with new situations, subjects, and people. I speak various languages. I'm numerate and literate. (Feel free at this stage to add in any attribute, however banal. It's often your unnoticed, undervalued, and unrewarded personal qualities that can make all the difference. Furthermore, this is an exercise in building the self-confidence we all need to make the changes necessary to move on in life, so be generous in your approval of yourself!) On the minus side, my IT skills are a bit sketchy—so, sign up for an intensive course. Put personal finances and admin in order. Make a will. Tidy up the papers on my metaphorical desk.

Next, it's worth considering the environment in which you currently find yourself. Few people live a life of glorious isolation. Most of you will have other people and commitments that are going to be affected by your decisions. Ask yourself which external factors you need to consider when planning to repot. Are these factors manageable or genuinely insurmountable constraints?

1.   Who are the key stakeholders (family, friends, dependents, teammates, colleagues, employer, employees . . .)

who have a legitimate interest in, or who will be directly affected by, your decision to effect changes in your life?

2. Make an honest assessment of your own domestic, work, health, and financial situation. Is your repotting plan realistic in the context of all these considerations? If not, are you prepared to take risks, and, if so, who else is required to buy into the effects/accept the consequences of your risk-taking?

3. Do you feel free to discuss the issues involved with the key people in your life? If not, why not? Perhaps this reluctance to communicate your feelings openly and honestly is part of the reason why you've ended up feeling potbound?

4. Do your responsibilities genuinely prevent you from making the changes you want to make in your life? Or are you using people and commitments as an excuse to absolve yourself from the effort required to undertake the next stage of your own personal development?

It's not a question of making a value judgment about how you elect to lead your life, and it's often unfair to judge the wisdom or correctness of a personal decision by its outcome. What might prove an insurmountable barrier to change for one person (e.g., the need to stay put and provide for a dependant partner and family) might not necessarily constrain another. Who can tell how these decisions will pan out in the future? We're forever being fed inspirational tales culminating in unimaginably successful outcomes when the people involved appear to have made the correct call. Quite rightly, we celebrate visionary entrepreneurs such as Sir James Dyson, individuals who threw in the benefits of a steady job to follow their dreams and ended up multimillionaires. We read far fewer stories about people who might have been equally visionary and entrepreneurial but, for want of good luck, good timing, or the right support, ended up in the unemployment line with a trail of financial failure and domestic distress following in their wake.

In my own case, and arguably one of the major benefits of advanced middle age, I was no longer constrained by the demands of dependents, as my daughter had long since flown the nest and was now well on her personal and professional way. Since activities such as scaling Everest without oxygen, free soloing up El Capitan, and BASE jumping from Norway's Troll Wall did not feature high on my bucket list, I felt that my health was robust enough to cope with the sort of repotting exercise that I might want to undertake. And in terms of cash, since

I wasn't exactly intending to mount an expedition to discover the lost world of Atlantis, I reckoned that I could find the financial wherewithal to execute whatever my next repotting plan might involve. Having cleared the decks and done the groundwork, I felt that I'd freed up enough headspace to consider the next move more carefully.

FIND WORKAROUNDS

At this point you may well start thinking that you'll never be able to overcome the morass of external factors now cropping up, bearing down, and generally boxing you in. Take a moment to reflect. As the Serenity Prayer reminds us, there are certain things that you can never control or remove. For over a decade, I had a financial interest in a construction company. Quite how I ended up being involved in a business about which I knew absolutely nothing need not detain us here, but after a few years watching with unashamed voyeurism from the sidelines, I decided to become more actively involved. Kitted out with my own hard hat and ISO-regulation metal-toed shoes, I soon found myself addicted to the energy of active building sites, to the guilty pleasures of packets of on-site snacks, and to the gypsum-chalky smell of freshly plastered walls. None of this compared, however, to the intense satisfaction of watching the process as a project made its way from drawing board to dream home. One thing I noticed, though, was that the professionals specializing in the construction of new-build properties enjoyed a relatively easy ride compared with those working on the refurbishment of an existing property. Dealing with legacy issues is always a far more challenging proposition—much more aligned to the repotting process—but all the more rewarding for it. The key, as I learned, is to figure out how to work around or, failing that, how to work with any given problem.

When it comes to repotting, a good design plan will be required to deal with existing immovable features. Genuinely immovable features might include considerations such as your own physical age, genetic predisposition, and chronic health issues, which, although capable of mitigation, cannot be fundamentally altered. However, many *apparently* immovable features often benefit from closer inspection to establish whether they are *genuinely* immovable. Since time immemorial, for example, the problem of poor eyesight effectively precluded millions of us from livelihoods, activities, and hobbies that we might have wished to pursue. Nowadays, thanks to spectacular developments in the field of ophthalmology, a relatively simple cataract operation can restore excellent vision to otherwise seriously visually impaired individuals. For vast numbers of people across the globe, an apparently immovable barrier can be made to disappear with the help of a thirty-minute operation. Whether genuine or apparent (and it's up to you to decide which kind of barrier is truly which and to deal with each accordingly), existing features need somehow to be accommodated in your repotting life plan. Occasionally the very thought of these immovable features may inhibit you from getting to work on a new design. Resist the temptation to become fixated on the problematic feature and instead find a way of working around it. If you don't, your dream home will never be built as you persist in digging that big, black hole.

A recent piece of research investigated the different ways in which men and women traditionally attack the challenge of applying for a job. If the job specification contains ten key criteria, the research suggested, a woman will look at it, decide that she has only eight out of ten of those criteria, and will therefore not feel competent enough to apply. A man, by contrast, will look at the same job spec, decide that he has six out of ten of the relevant criteria, and apply for the position confident that he can pick up the missing four while working on the job. My advice for repotters is to adopt the can-do attitude of the archetypal male jobseeker. Whereas potbound people end up stuck in a rut, repotters are prepared to work around any impediments that get in their way. Instead of concentrating on what they cannot do, they stand back and turn the whole problem on its head to establish what *can* be managed.

This is not to say that taking stock is a time for delusional optimism, but nor is it a time for paralyzing pessimism. In the world of regular repotters, where optimism is almost a moral duty, the attitude of pure pessimism gets an understandably bad rap. As a realistic compromise, however, I'd like to make the case for an attitude of *constructive pessimism*. With its associated feelings of confusion and frustration, constructive pessimism can be a positive sign. Discontentment can sometimes be the fuel that keeps you moving forward on the right track. It can also be the signal that alerts you to the fact that you're onto something worth pursuing.

Let me explain. Most of you will have experienced the occasional thrill of getting something absolutely right, an achievement somewhere along the success spectrum between the soufflé that rises to perfection and the vaccination that saves the world. More often, however, you probably experience that nagging feeling that you could have done things better, which, in turn, spurs you on to try harder. Taken to extremes, this commitment to improvement can lead to the curse of perfectionism and the refusal to accept anything short of absolutely impeccable. Few individuals are made of such unforgivingly stern stuff, but most of us do want to do the very best we can. When it comes to deciding which attitude to adopt, therefore, it may seem that you're confronted with a confusing fork in the road.

Do you take the pessimist's path of least resistance, engage in jobs for which you're overqualified, confine yourself to challenges where you're guaranteed success, and engage only with the sort of people who neither stretch nor motivate you? It's an easy road to follow, but the chances are that you'll find it flat and boring. You may protect yourself against the low points in life, but you'll be sacrificing the thrill of the highs. Or do you opt for the delusional optimist's path and spend your life forever in search of the ever-receding perfectionism of eternally sunlit uplands?

I suggest you do neither. For me, the constructive pessimism approach, a modified version of perfectionism for the slacker in search of the suboptimal sublime, seems like a sensible compromise. If, for instance, you start your small business because of a burning desire to be as rich as Mark Zuckerberg, Jeff Bezos, or Elon Musk, then your business will always be a failure in your own eyes if you never reach those dizzying heights. If, on the contrary, you start your small business with the profound conviction that you're creating a product or a service that's useful, exciting, or fills a need in your community, then your chances of success will be considerably higher. Too often we seek inspiration in other people's outstandingly successful outcomes. Instructive though these examples may be, especially when associated with the protagonist's warts-and-all backstory, it's more helpful to focus on finding what truly moves and motivates you, however humble that might sound initially. Who would ever have believed, for example, that a website started by an irate mother who'd endured a particularly lousy vacation in Florida with some decidedly disgruntled kids would develop into Mumsnet, the highly influential parents' network now feared and courted by British politicians of every political persuasion? Understand what gets *you* going, pushes *your* buttons, or motivates *you*; therein lie the contours of *your* own bespoke design plan.

FIGURE OUT WHAT MAKES YOU HAPPY

Once you have built up a realistic assessment of who you are and where you find yourself, it's time to consider what kind of new future would make you happy, or at least satisfied or fulfilled. For many people this is one of the hardest questions of all, but it is one worth asking at any stage of your life. When the eighty-year-old parents of a friend of mine decided to divorce, their entire family was left feeling totally sandbagged. None of them could understand it. All they had ever witnessed was a couple who seemed perfectly happy and who rubbed along in such gentle and supportive companionship that they even finished one another's sentences. And yet, when my friend talked to her mother about the divorce, she belatedly came to realize that this wonderful, elderly lady had been feeling potbound and clinging onto a moribund marriage for the best part of a decade. It was only when the last grandchild, whom she'd been helping to look after, went off to preschool that she finally found the courage to ask herself what it was that *she* wanted. And, as it turned out, this did not involve spending the rest of her life with the man she had married over half a century before. For women in particular, the repotting process might be the very first time in your adult life that you are asking yourself what it is that you *want* to do. Not what you *can* do. Not what you *should* do. Not what your parents/partner/children *want* you to do. And not what society *expects* you to do. Whatever your circumstances, before you start trying to construct a design brief for your future repotted life, let me offer two overall pieces of advice:

Make it yours

Too often, at this stage, you might be tempted to copy another person's design, which, however appropriate and successful for them, may well end up being a complete catastrophe when applied to your pot or plot. If I hadn't signed a filing cabinet full of nondisclosure agreements, I'd happily regale you with the disaster stories of various homeowners I came across in the construction industry. Dazzled by a well-produced portfolio, they would decide to put their prospective dream home into the hands of some prima donna designer, who would insist on delivering some much vaunted "signature-style" design without any "interference" from the paying customer. While it worked for those clients who had punctiliously sought out a designer whose aesthetic aligned precisely with their own, there were unfortunately many others who ended up dissatisfied with what was essentially someone else's perfect dream home. When it comes to repotting your life, neither off-the-peg nor bespoke solutions created by other people will do the job for you. You have to put the effort in to act as your own designer.

It's the same when it comes to dealing with other people's opinions. A few months ago, I came across a man who'd spent almost ten years of his life engaged in the demanding study, tough exams, and grueling training required to qualify as an ER doctor—only to discover, after all his efforts, that this career path wasn't for him. He had fallen victim to the classic mistake of following received wisdom without ever forming his own opinion. Highfliers like him were *supposed* to get high-flying degrees like medicine, and the career prospects were excellent. At least, that's what his teachers had always told him, and that's what he'd ended up believing was important. The trouble was that it was only once he'd qualified that this doctor began seriously considering what truly mattered to him—and it wasn't spending the rest of his professional life triaging, resuscitating, and intubating desperately ill patients in an emergency room. Now, a further ten years later, and having followed the call of his inner voice, he has repotted as a Buddhist monk. He is continuing his mission to heal, but in his own way and outside the confines of traditional medicine.

Many of us are influenced and sidetracked by illusions about how best we should lead our lives. Some are due to parental and societal expectations, such as the traditional pressure to find a responsible job, settle down, get married, and have children—"the full catastrophe," as the title character describes it in the comedy drama *Zorba the Greek*. We're also bombarded with a constant stream of carefully curated and commercially motivated images of what a "happy" or "successful" life is supposed to look like. Resist the temptation to drink the Kool-Aid. You may be lucky enough to find a moment of temporary happiness in a pot of probiotic yogurt or a surgically reconstructed version of a Kardashian-esque rear end, but the chances of finding sustained fulfillment in other people's designs or derrieres tend to be vanishingly small.

It's worth taking time to interrogate some of the unquestioned certainties that have informed your life so far and establish whether they're true or illusory. Behaviors and reactions deriving from deeply rooted convictions including religious beliefs, political persuasion, or unchallenged notions about your own place in society may not withstand the icy blast of some serious scrutiny. Try reading, listening to, and engaging with ideas from as wide a range of different people as possible. In other words, get out of the filter bubble where your own preconceived ideas are endlessly reinforced by commentators who think and act exactly as you do. If you never extract yourself from your echo chamber of minimes, you'll find it impossible to assess and reverse the effects of what's already gone wrong and left you feeling potbound. And if you don't spend some time coming to terms with that realization, you'll end up baking the same old mistakes and misconceptions into your new design. Give a particular grilling to the limiting beliefs you hold that you've never thought to challenge: anything and everything from "People my age don't go back to college" to "I'm too insignificant to make a difference." Then look around and find individuals whose actions are proving your own limiting beliefs quite wrong.

While you won't be able to follow their precise examples, at least some elements of their stories might encourage you to rethink what could be possible for you and to discard any ill-conceived notions that have thus far kept you trapped and firmly "in your place." You'll feel energized to dig up your illusions, root them out, and dispose of them in an environmentally friendly fashion before you go any further.

As you embark on this next phase of your repotting journey, even the deeply ingrained and almost universally shared notion of deferred gratification also needs to be challenged. The illusion that if you work hard, you'll eventually be successful and happy is a notion that is universally and endlessly peddled. You've probably found, however, to your continual disappointment, that the goalposts keep moving, the fruits of your successes are never quite ripe, and the promised land remains forever tantalizingly out of reach. In the process, you may develop a six-pack of struggle muscles, but your happiness muscle may well end up atrophying from lack of use. It's time to plan a life that affords you a greater degree of happiness, fulfillment, or purpose—not at some indeterminate rainbow's end, but at every step along the way.

Avoid the passion trap

I've often envied the life of the professional sportsman and woman. These, after all, are individuals who are lucky enough to be able to combine their love for a sport with a means of making a living: an enviably gratifying alignment of passion, purpose, and paycheck. Find a job that you love, so the old saying goes, and you'll never have to work again. Many repotters are trying to accomplish just that—to find something to do with their lives that they can feel "passionate" about. Indeed, it's the perceived "lack of passion" in their current lives that has often left them feeling the need for change.

Personally, I think the way we define "passion" has led us all into a terrible trap. It's a concept so laden with connotations of heightened emotion that few folk feel that they could ever aspire to its dramatic extremes. When you hear the word "passion," you immediately start to think of all those tragically destructive love stories: Romeo and Juliet, Abelard and Héloïse, Donald Trump and Donald Trump. Or you may contemplate incomparably indefatigable campaigners in the mold of Mother Teresa, Mahatma Gandhi, and Nelson Mandela. When you're led to consider "passion" in those terms, it's hardly surprising that your own daily interests and efforts seem depressingly lackluster.

And then you start to ask yourself how you can possibly find "passion" in an everyday life of table-waiting, shelf-stacking, or diaper-changing. Pity the poor students who, at eighteen, are expected to identify a passion that will supposedly inspire them not only during but way beyond the dreaming spires of higher education and throughout a forty-year professional life. I believe that it's high time to expand the common understanding of this damagingly restrictive concept so that everyone can participate in life's passion play. How about reframing the concept of "passion" and considering it instead as the *attitude* that informs your ostensibly less grandiose and glamorous actions and endeavors? Once you do that, you'll realize that it's not necessarily the job itself, but the attitude you bring to all the ancillary aspects of it that can genuinely add up to "passion."

I once had an early-morning slot on BBC breakfast television that involved scanning the morning papers, compiling a digest of the most interesting and amusing stories, and performing my scripted piece for a camera. My modest efforts to improve the gaiety of a grumpily awakening nation involved a 4 a.m. alarm call and an arrival at the BBC's White City headquarters by 5 a.m. at the latest. In short, a breakfast television slot was grim, but at least it left you with the rest of the day free to feel absolutely wrecked. At that time, the BBC news department had a wonderful tea lady. Well into her sixties, if not seventies, she not only knew everyone around by name, but she even knew everyone's early-morning breakfast preferences. Whenever I turned up at my allotted hot desk at the appointed godforsaken hour, I would find my English breakfast tea with milk and no sugar and my croissant with butter but no jam already waiting for me. Indefatigably cheerful, she went about her business with a maternal kindliness that made everyone feel at home and took the edge off all those gruesome early-morning starts.

One day, in one of their classic "hitting the target and missing the point" cost-cutting exercises, the bean counters at the BBC decided that the tea lady was an item of expenditure that could easily be deleted from the budget and her function assumed by a series of automated tea and coffee dispensers. The reaction was immediate. Within hours, a petition had been signed by all those whose lives had been improved by their daily dealings with the tea lady—and that meant everyone in the building plus anyone else who ever visited it.

News headlines were soon circulating that threatened a "storm in a teacup" and left BBC management in no doubt that they had picked the wrong target. No one gives awards to tea ladies, and their official approval ratings are never charted, but for me, the overwhelming reaction to the idea of laying off the tea lady was recognition of the right kind of "passion"—it had nothing to do with a deep and abiding love for all things tea-related, but the pride and pleasure our early-morning ministering angel took in doing her work to the highest possible standard. That's how I think we should redefine "passion."

WATCH OUT FOR AN ATTACK OF "THE NEVERS"

So, what's the best way to figure out where you want to be? It was around the age of sixty-five that I first recognized my most recent potbound predicament. It was flagged by an acute dose of what is sometimes called "The Nevers." Common symptoms of this malaise include the sudden, incandescent insight that if you don't do something pretty quickly, then you'll never do it at all, and for some reason I found myself focusing on the fact that I'd never in my life had a gap year. In search of answers, I did what most people nowadays would do and googled "gap years for geriatrics." I now realize, of course, that I was making a common mistake. A gap year is just a temporary break from normality. Like having your hair restyled or rearranging your living room furniture, the difference may be obvious to others, but the reality is that it's only superficial. It may be a change, but it's not a lasting or meaningful transformation. There is no shortage of palm-fringed beach advertisements inviting us to take time out from our lives to recharge our batteries. Relaxing as it may be to drink daiquiris while diving with dolphins at dawn—or whatever the latest marketing mash-up is promoting—such temporary respites have limited long-term impact. You may return home from an extended break feeling more energized, but experience has probably taught you that the effects will wear off even before the gold-plating on the dodgy Rolex you bought from the bloke on the beach.

Something else I noticed when I was scanning the results of my Google search was that the vast majority of the activities suggested seemed based on the assumption that older people are interested only in leisure activities and the frenzied pursuit of a second childhood. In affluent societies, entire industries have grown up around older people assiduously working their way through frantically compiled and checked-off bucket lists as a way of passing their time in God's waiting room. There seems to be a sense that people of a certain age have nothing more to offer, that they are superfluous to society and should just content themselves with a life of relatively trivial pastimes. Although that clearly works well for some people, many of us are still looking for something more than the putting green of eternity, endlessly working on our handicap. I swiftly realized that

I didn't just want a gap year. I didn't want to set sail and go gentle into that dark Costa Geriatrica night. I needed to find a new purpose even if that required a more demanding transition to accede to some other, still meaningful, stage of life. To identify what I needed, I realized that I was going to have to refine my search even further.

If you ever find yourself at a similar set of crossroads, it's helpful to take time to reflect on a few questions along the following lines:

1. Think of a period in your life when you felt truly enthusiastic and engaged. What were you doing?

2. Can you think of any missed or wasted opportunities that you now regret and that you'd like to revisit or redress?

3. What are you waiting for? A star from the east? If not now, when?

My own answers came as something of a revelation, even to me. I found myself recalling the enthusiasm and engagement of my years at college, the fun of learning and the excitement of exploring new subjects in the company of smart and supportive people. To my shame, I also recalled the eons of time wasted in search of the meaning of life in the dregs of some cheap and nasty wine. If only I could be a student again, but without the acne and the adolescent angst. If only I could relive such a transformational period but with the benefit of hindsight and an eye to the future—the Janus of repotters!

Once you've run through your own list, take a look at your answers and try to find a common thread that links what you do well, what you love, and where you've previously been successful. Is there a recurrent leitmotif that connects the parts of your life and career that you have found most enjoyable and fulfilling? This golden thread may not be obvious at first sight, but on closer inspection, you may find that it revolves around something intangible, such as your gift for problem-solving, supporting others, or just being the person who always manages to make everyone else laugh or feel better about themselves. With a little patience, you'll start to see some patterns and answers emerging from life's often kaleidoscopic jumble.

At this stage of my own repotting process, I found unexpected help from the diaries that I've been keeping on and off almost since the day I learned how to write. Nowadays, pop psychologists have elevated this humble "Dear Diary" practice to the intellectually far higher status of "journaling." Whatever label is appended to the process, my own untrammeled mental meanderings have always roamed widely to embrace everything from intimate feelings to extensive to-do lists, with an occasional excursion into character assassination thrown in. When I was considering my own repotting journey, I came across one long-lost, dog-eared diary that dated back to my early school days. What a revelation! If only I'd been able then to interpret the significance of my own only dimly apprehended perceptions. Descriptions of the classmates I'd loved and who'd made me laugh and the mean ones I detested and who'd tried to make others cry; thoughts on the subjects that I'd most enjoyed (French and Latin) and the classes that I'd always dreaded (geography and physical education—no wonder I'm still incapable of finding my way to the gym); a catalog of events and places that had filled me with childlike joy and the situations that had left me feeling miserable. This battered old repository of infantile insights contained the clues for personal happiness that I'd spent my adult life ignoring but was now again ready to decipher. Rereading the childish scribbles of my schooldays, the clues became clear. Identify what engages and excites you. Armed with that understanding, pursue those activities that allow you to play to your strengths and interests. This, in turn, will boost your energy levels and help you engage in whatever it is you want to try next.

As a quick aside, we've already discussed the benefits of keeping a diary to help you identify your patterns. A diary can also be a very useful way of keeping track of what's working for you and what isn't, what you enjoy and what you don't, what gives you energy and what drains it away. Here's an entry I made in my diary some time ago: "Long phone call with X who wouldn't stop whining about Y (her appalling boss). *Plus ça change!* Felt washed out by the end of it. Don't take calls from X when trying to work!" And here's another entry: "Salsa lesson with Diego, over-the-top Cuban teacher recommended by Z. Laughed a lot. Says it would really help if I could distinguish left from right in any language." A diary helps you track the effects of your activities and interactions on your energy levels. You can then fine-tune and improve your daily life without the need to make massive structural changes.

PRIORITIZE THE THINGS THAT MATTER

In an effort to accommodate the key areas of most people's lives and lifestyles, many contemporary garden designers split the available outdoor space into a series of discrete areas. Some people want an area in which to entertain and have fun, others a place where they can be quiet and relax; some want a productive patch where they can grow food; others need a space where the children can play or that's devoted to fitness and exercise. Similarly, when designing your repotted future, it's helpful to decide how to make best use of the space in your own notional garden.

Of course, it's one thing to divide a garden up into discrete areas, but it's quite another to do that with your future life—with all of its complex, multilayered, overlapping, interrelated areas of activity. To overcome this, try thinking of life as a jar to be filled with a combination of rocks, pebbles, and sand. The rocks represent the fundamental, nonnegotiable elements of your life; the pebbles, the significant but less crucial issues; and the sand, the more trivial, "nice-to-have" nonessentials. To put together a well-organized jar of life, you have to put the rocks in first, followed by the pebbles, and then pour in the sand so that it can arrange itself into any remaining spaces. Try filling the jar in reverse order and you'll find that the sand commandeers its own very definite layer of space. Add pebbles and you'll find that the jar is almost full and you no longer have the available space required to accommodate the all-important rocks. If you apply the same reverse jar-filling routine to your life, you'll end up sacrificing your most important concerns to relatively minor pursuits. So how does your jar of life stack up?

1. What are the current rocks in your life? These key elements may well change over time but will probably include your most important personal relationships,

your work, and the attention that you need to devote to maintaining your overall health and well-being.

2. What are the current pebbles in your life? These secondary concerns may include, for instance, your circle of good friends; your network of close colleagues; pastimes or interests that involve serious commitment.

3. What is the sand in your life? These are all the tertiary activities such as shopping, casual socializing, entertainment, undemanding hobbies, travel . . .

Of course, the issues that you classify as rocks, pebbles, or sand will change depending on your stage in life and focus of interest, so it's useful to reappraise your categories from time to time. Of course, there has to be some wiggle room, as the rock, pebble, sand stratification can't always be rigidly adhered to on a daily basis. Furthermore, during periods of change or transition, you may have to allocate vastly different weightings to certain activities. For those nearing retirement, for example, the all-consuming "work" rock may be relegated to pebble or even sand significance, while the sand of volunteering may be elevated to pebble or even rock status in the hierarchy of your life jar.

LOOK FOR IDEAS AND INSPIRATION

So far we have looked at who you are, what your current situation is, what makes you happy, and what you consider important. These are the specifications for your new repotted life—something along the lines of a wish list that you might compile when you're looking for a new apartment or house. Now it's time to start looking at what's available out there that might fit the bill. Quite what that might be will be different for each and every one of you, but allow me to suggest some general advice on how you might go about finding it.

Embrace your curiosity

Planning to repot can sometimes make you feel like one of those soon-to-be-released long-term prisoners who've become so institutionalized that they have no idea how to exploit their newfound freedom. The trick is to look at this new start the same way that a two-year-old would—not with fear but with unalloyed wonder. Spending some time in the company of one of these tiny adventurers with their insistent questions of "Why?" may be enough to test the patience of a saint, but it does make you appreciate how dramatically our own capacity for embracing possibility and opportunity has shrunk as we grow older.

It's time to start asking questions again! The more input and options you garner, no matter how far-fetched they first appear, the more enabled you'll feel to move away from old, circumscribed ideas and plan something that not only works for you but is also authentically yours. When I started designing my own repotted life, I began by considering a course in coding. How did that happen? Because I kept asking myself the question "Why?"

Why? Because I'm interested in languages, and coding is a language.

Why? Because I keep hearing people talking about it and it sounds like a powerful tool. Why? Because I know nothing about this Brave New World and I don't want to be left stuck in the Ice Age . . .

One web search led to another and another and another. Conversations with family and friends opened up new possibilities. Suddenly, ideas and inspiration seemed to be popping up all over the place—in books, magazines, the internet, and radio and television programs. Within a year, by following what I found interesting, asking questions, and embracing my curiosity, my initial thoughts about a coding language course had morphed into something completely different. There's no knowing where this process will end up once you suspend your adult judgment and allow your curiosity to lead wherever serendipity may take you.

Reach out!

I wouldn't normally suggest a TV box set as an optimal tool for self-development, but I'm forced to make an exception in the case of *The Last Dance*, the totally engrossing miniseries I chanced on when it was being streamed on Netflix. A no-holds-barred American sports documentary, *The Last Dance* charts the success story of the Chicago Bulls in the early 1990s and of the legendary Michael Jordan's amazing career within that organization. One of the greatest basketball players of all time, Jordan was blessed with extraordinary focus and determination, and his leaping ability, prolific scoring, and genius in performing slam dunks from the free throw line gave him every right to expect a career generously garlanded with success. So far, so cliché! The truly interesting story begins, however, with Jordan's gradual realization that, no matter how outstanding a player he might be, he would never lead a winning team until he learned how to recognize and rely on the talents of the other, often less obviously stellar, players around him.

Resilience and self-reliance are key attributes for any repotter, and there will always be issues that you have to work through by yourself. There are far more times, however, when you're going to need the help and support of others. We human beings are pack animals. We don't tend to thrive on being alone; neither do we achieve the best results without a supportive group of people around us. When I think of some of the extremely complex projects that my old construction company completed over the years, the people who come to mind are a wildly eclectic group. Diverse trades including electricians, glaziers, masons, welders, sheet metal workers, roofers, scaffolders, painters, decorators, carpet fitters, bricklayers, laborers, and hod carriers all worked together and, in concert, painstakingly delivered all those challenging and multifaceted projects. Likewise, by drawing on a wide range of experience and expertise, you're far more likely to find useful new perspectives, ideas, and inspiration about your repotted future. Individuals who rightly pride themselves on their self-reliance often find it difficult to reach out and ask for help. But even the most accomplished designers in the world need the input and expertise of a supportive community to turn their plans into reality. How you design your life should always be *your* decision. But your repotting plan, like all the best designs, is best accomplished with team effort.

Keep it simple

As you amass ideas and inspiration for your new direction in life, try not to fall into the trap of casting your net evermore widely. In a consumer-focused world awash with apparently infinite variety, the curse of excessive choice can often be paralyzing. A highly respected journalist I know spent a period during her early career learning about the mail-order business that predated our current craze for online shopping. The insights she gained from selling a range of fruit-flavored panties in cans (don't ask, but they sold in heaps!) to readers of the *Sun*, the UK's most popular tabloid, stood her in good stead when she subsequently became editor of a well-known women's magazine. Whenever a mail-order promotion for ladies' dresses, tops, or trousers was being advertised, she knew that readers should be given no more than three choices of size (small, medium, or large) and three possible colors from which to pick (usually black, navy blue, or beige). When the publication stuck to this simple prescription, the customer response was terrific and the orders flooded in. If the magazine ever departed from its restricted 3 × 3 range of options, prospective customers became overwhelmed by the confusion of possible permutations. Faced with an overload of choice, many potential customers were incapable of reaching a decision, and sales were substantially lower.

Try designing your life like a mail-order promotion. Keep referring back to the Rocks—Pebbles—Sand life jar that you've established and ask yourself whether and how each new possibility works within that three-level hierarchy. Try and identify the three ideas that most appeal to you and concentrate on those so that you can eventually make a final, well-informed, and realistically manageable choice. And remember—what you're focusing on at this stage is just a possible destination. Don't worry too much about how you're going to get there—we'll deal with that in chapter 3.

WHEN THE STUDENT IS READY, THE MASTER WILL APPEAR

Just like when you plant a seed in the ground, nothing may seem to happen for quite some time, but while you're planning to repot, there's already crucial transformational work going on beneath the surface. In my own case, I'd been vaguely wondering about the next phase of my life for a couple of years, and actively researching the options for around twelve months. However, the catalyst for the final plunge involved my daughter, Alexandra, the most important rock in my jar. After an initial career in investment banking, she decided on a complete change of direction and applied for the MBA course at Stanford University's world-renowned

Graduate School of Business. Around the same time, I heard from old friends whom I'd known since our children were at school together. They were about to relocate to California, having been accepted in a groundbreaking program—as it happened, also at Stanford. My ears pricked up. Talk about serendipity! Every year, they told me, the Distinguished Careers Institute offered individuals from all walks of life and from all over the world the opportunity of a yearlong residential program of personal renewal and community engagement. The program was designed to consider how a return to higher education in midlife might impact individuals, institutions, and communities. In addition, the DCI was hoping to assess the value of intergenerational learning, teaching, and mentoring between university students and mature individuals with diverse career and professional experience.

Nowhere in my research had I found any program quite so inspirational and international in its substance, scope, and intent. Designed to foster a close-knit community of mature individuals—very different in background but united in their desire to learn, change, and grow— the description of the program seemed to check all my boxes. From the moment I heard about it, I absolutely knew that the DCI was the right road for me. On the East Coast, Harvard's celebrated Executive Leadership

Program was teaching people how to lead major corporations. Over on the West Coast, Stanford's DCI was encouraging people to lead meaningful lives. I had no idea how I'd manage to get myself selected for the program, but I knew I had three unassailable advantages: enormous enthusiasm, total ignorance, and a burning desire to go. Suddenly, I felt eighteen again, buzzing with hope and determination. I'd done the groundwork, I'd created my plan, now it was time to take the plunge. I went ahead and applied.

MAKE YOUR CHOICE!

When asked the question "What makes a good general?" Emperor Napoleon is reported to have replied, "A good general is a general who makes a decision." Once you have pulled together three or four possible directions for your repotted future, it's vital that you don't spend the rest of eternity agonizing over making the "absolutely right" decision. Despite its endless peddling by popular music, romantic literature, and the movie industry, there is no such thing as an absolute "Mr. or Mrs. Right." No torso-clinging damp-shirted Mr. Darcy is likely to emerge from a conveniently situated lake to sweep us off our feet and assume the mantle of the one and only life partner who will ensure that we live happily ever after. (Feel free to insert your own equivalent male/female fantasies here.) Likewise, there is no one single plan that will afford you a fulfilled and purposeful repotted life. There are always multiple options on offer. The key is to decide on your best option and then move on. Don't keep endlessly rehashing the issues.

Perhaps even worse than agonizing over a decision is our tendency not to make any decision at all. It is all too easy to convince yourself that no matter how unsatisfactory your current, familiar situation, it's still far better than an unknown future. But what you suffer when you stay stuck in fear is almost always more damaging than facing that fear and acting decisively to deal with it. Back in the days of the Flintstones, it was obviously far wiser to remain huddled up in the cave than to sally forth at night to hunt down a carnivore-based breakfast. Despite humanity's enormous technological progress, human beings have never fully shaken off those very rational atavistic attitudes to unknown dangers. Admittedly, we've made some progress— if we hadn't eventually faced those fears and chased those mammoths, we'd never have made it out of those caves at all—but the remnants of this evolutionary wiring explain why our brains function like Velcro for negative experiences and like Teflon for positive ones. I can hardly recall any one of the tens of thousands of car journeys that I've undertaken without incident, but I can vividly remember the time I hit a displaced traffic cone on a hairpin turn on a cliff in the south of France, careered out of control across the road, and but for a robust barrier would have ended up plummeting to my certain death into a romantically rugged ravine. It was truly terrifying, but I can't allow the infinitesimal chances of meeting another rogue traffic cone on some imaginary hairpin turn to inhibit me from ever driving again. So what if your last relationship was with a Klingon camouflaged in human disguise! You can't allow that to mean that the next man or woman you meet is going to be another emotional extraterrestrial. However grim past experiences may have been, the Velcro of Doom has no place in your next repotting design! To give yourself the final push, try experimenting with the following exercise:

1. Is this plan consistent with my values and priorities?

2. I recognize that I'm feeling unsure about some of the details, but do I feel right about the key features of this plan?

3. I've done the due diligence to the best of my ability. Can I now promise to give this plan my very best shot?

4. Can I also promise not to beat myself up if things don't work out? If things go pear-shaped, can I promise just to reflect, learn the lessons, and move on?

The simple truth is that you can never eliminate all the risks associated with repotting, and you can never foresee the final outcome. What you can do, however, is actively decide to liberate yourself from your buried irrational and atavistic emotions. Find yourself a quiet place. Pause and consider the three options that you have outlined for yourself. Each one offers a well-informed, rationally determined destination for your future life. Three possible futures—all of them better than your current life. Pick one! Now start figuring out how you're going to get yourself there.

SUMMARY

1. Take stock of who you are, your strengths and weaknesses, your successes and failures, and your current situation in life.

2. Understand what you can and cannot change and what you can work around. Adopt an attitude of constructive pessimism.

3. Analyze what makes you feel happy or fulfilled. Trust the path taken by your own imagination, research, and thinking. Don't get trapped into pursuing too narrow or too grandiose a definition of passion.

4. Prioritize what matters to you—the rocks, pebbles, and sand that you want to fit into your own jar of life.

5. Cast your net widely, but not eternally, for ideas on where you want to be. Allow your curiosity free rein. Reach out to others for advice and inspiration.

6. Whittle down your ideas to three or four viable repotting destinations, control your anxieties, and make an active, informed choice. Decide, don't slide!

PULLING UP
THE ROOTS

How do you prepare to end one phase of your life and commit to your new repotted future?

Since its publication in 1937, J. R. R. Tolkien's fantasy novel *The Hobbit* has delighted generations of adults and children. Set in a fictional universe, the novel follows the quest of the modest, reserved, and home-loving Bilbo Baggins, our eponymous hobbit. Uprooted from the circumscribed comfort of his familiar, rural surroundings in the Shire, Bilbo finds himself engaged on an often terrifying journey. At every turn, the unlikely hero is confronted with new and ever-more-demanding challenges. Discovering hitherto untapped inner strengths and drawing on his wits and common sense, Bilbo somehow finds the resources to overcome all the trials and tribulations before him and, in so doing, acquires deeper levels of maturity, expertise, and wisdom. By the end of this epic tale of heroism and growth, Bilbo returns home to the Shire as a wiser, nobler, and infinitely better hobbit.

While Bilbo's tale of personal and spiritual development remains relevant for all repotters, most of us would be ill-advised to rely on mere chance or the expectation of magical intervention to help us navigate our next steps. Bilbo's classic "hero's journey" is an adventure story, with all the thrills and spills generally associated with that genre. Striking out into new territory will often involve the excitement and anxiety of an adventure, but a realistic repotting journey requires the planning of an expedition, not the fortuitousness of fantasy, if it's going to stand a reasonable chance of success. Of course, like many expeditions, including the voyage of discovery led by that compelling yet controversial explorer, Christopher Columbus, you may not necessarily end up where you initially planned to go. After all, Columbus was trying to reach Asia from Spain via a westward route when he ended up "discovering" the Bahamas and large swaths of Central and South America instead. No matter! The discovery of the "New World" was a remarkable achievement, and much of the project's undeniable success was down to Columbus's ability to join the disparate dots of his own life up to the date he eventually set sail. It was on the basis of those experiences, insights, and expertise that he was able to formulate a realistic and credible, albeit ambitious, plan for his future voyage of exploration. Brought up in Italy with a childhood and adolescence spent helping out at his father's cheese stall, Columbus might not seem, at first sight, to have benefited from the classic derring-do of a buccaneering background. However, by the time he began dreaming up plans for the New World, he had already experienced at least one radical repotting by joining up as a seaman in the Portuguese merchant marine. It was here that Columbus acquired the skill set, confidence, and seafaring curiosity required for his remarkable expedition. Furthermore, and like any good repotter, he did his homework as assiduously as anyone could in the 1490s and set about studying *The Travels of Marco Polo*, Pierre d'Ailly's *Imago Mundi*, and Ptolemy's estimation of the circumference of the globe. Despite a few glitches and reversals, this combination of planning, pluck, and professional credentials paid off at last and, with a favorable wind and the backing of the king and queen of Spain (always helpful to have royalty in your corner), Columbus was on his way.

Whether you're comfortably potbound like Bilbo Baggins and suddenly catapulted into change or actively searching for the next move into unknown territory in the manner of Christopher Columbus, the impetus to uproot from your current situation provides an opportunity for transformational growth. The downside is that uprooting always involves the wrench of separation, and this invariably feels uncomfortable. Keen gardeners will be aware of the folklore surrounding the mandrake, a hallucinogenic plant whose roots often resemble a human body and which, according to legend, cries out in agonizing pain when it is pulled from the earth. For some of us, uprooting can involve equally acute levels of distress, and it's helpful to recognize the toll that uprooting will probably take in the short term. Whether uprooting involves leaving a relationship, quitting a job, moving on from a generally unsatisfactory or outworn situation, or giving up a habitually negative pattern of behavior, the ultimate "mandrake moment" can often feel overwhelming.

THIS *WILL* HURT A BIT

It's important to emphasize that it is perfectly natural to feel discomfort and a degree of anxiety not only at the point of uprooting but throughout the entire process. First of all, we generally tend to start repotting when we are at a relatively low ebb—when we feel so undeniably unhappy, uncomfortable, or unfulfilled that there is no realistic option but to repot. The process itself is by definition an unsettling one, requiring not only a leap of faith but also an active decision to walk away from the relative security of our current life. It takes courage to leave a reality that we know well (even if it feels deeply unpleasant or unacceptable) and to venture out into uncharted and uncertain territory. It also requires energy at a point when we're likely to be feeling very short of that key resource. It's no wonder, then, that as an individual you might find yourself tempted to stay rooted where you are. Don't worry—you're not the only one!

Despite the advantage of enormous financial and personnel resources, even great businesses have been seriously wounded by the paralyzing fear of change. Business books are packed with case studies of once outstanding organizations (Kodak, Nokia, Xerox, Compaq, General Motors . . . the list goes on and on) whose leaders held on to the past, unable or unwilling to adapt to a new reality. But they are also filled with case studies of companies that have started and sometimes even achieved a significant degree of success, then altered and faced failure, tacked and changed course, acquired fresh insights, and emerged from this pivoting process far stronger and better geared up for a brighter future. You only have to read the case studies of Apple, Airbnb, Uber, and FedEx for a few examples of successful corporate repotters. In other words, you as an individual are far from alone in fearing change but, like the Apples of life, you must learn to embrace it if you're going to survive and thrive in an increasingly uncertain and volatile world.

On a visit to Yosemite in California, one of America's most outstanding national parks, I was fascinated to learn about the phenomenon of fire-activated seeds. An iconic symbol of Yosemite, the Mariposa Grove of giant sequoias is the largest remaining stand of these magnificent trees.

However, unlike the many species of trees unable to withstand the devastation of forest fires, the giant sequoias actually depend on the catalyst of fire to reproduce. In a classic case of ordeal by fire, the cones of the sequoia must go through the process of being burned at high temperatures in order to release their seeds. At the same time, the flames of the fire serve to clear the surrounding earth, which, in turn, allows the liberated seeds to germinate. Rather than causing the destruction of the tree, the fire ensures its procreation. In much the same way, crucible events in your life can result in breaking you open as opposed to breaking you apart. In other words, if the thought or the process of uprooting is making you feel anxious, don't take it as a sign that you are heading in the wrong direction. Try to draw inspiration from the giant sequoia and accept that tough transitions are often required for necessary, new growth.

MANAGING YOUR FEAR

To this time of uprooting, you'll no doubt bring with you whatever approach you've hit on in life so far for dealing with an ending. From the forensically clinical to the clumsily callous to the messily maudlin, we all develop our own responses to the closing of a door, invariably shaped by our past experiences. To make progress, it's crucial to be honest about your own habitual way of extracting yourself from uncomfortable or potbound situations. Do you act in an upfront manner with honesty, integrity, and an effort at clear communication? Or do you skulk around trying to ignore what's important like a coward afraid to engage head-on with the issues? Do you do your homework, arrive at an informed decision, and then act on it? Or does your tendency to prevaricate make Hamlet look like Indiana Jones? Ask yourself why you exit (or consistently fail to exit) the way you do. A bad exit is usually the result of fear, of an unwillingness to face up to the often highly emotional consequences of your decision to move on.

Even in far less dramatic or emotionally fraught situations, you may not even know why the prospect of a relatively simple exit fills you with overwhelming trepidation. If, for instance, you have buried or painful memories of loss or abandonment, the simple fact of acknowledging this history can help illuminate why you're finding the mere thought of a relatively simple uprooting so difficult. Nor do you have to have been physically abandoned on a doorstep at birth to feel the need to cling onto clearly potbound situations or relationships.

The only way of minimizing the fear that we all feel when letting go of the past is to prepare for the future as well as possible. "The more I practice, the luckier I get"—an aphorism ascribed to various outstanding golfers including Gary Player and Jerry Barber—helps point the way: "The more you prepare, the more confident you get." This insight, in turn, helps you to overcome your natural anxieties and concentrate on giving things your very best shot. Fail to plan and you plan to fail. Once you start thinking of repotting as an expedition, then the pain of departure—of the trauma involved in uprooting and setting sail—will be subsumed by your swift engagement in the subsequent steps that inevitably follow the action of casting off. Once again, try to concentrate on the things that you can control in order to mitigate your anxiety over those you can't. The following exercises may help move you through the worries associated with the uprooting phase by helping you concentrate on why you are repotting and keep you focused on your objectives:

How can you best describe your repotting project?

What is the purpose of what you're setting out to achieve? Will this be an exercise in physical improvement (such as losing weight, quitting smoking, reducing alcohol consumption, building physical fitness . . .) or in personal or professional development (e.g., acquiring an additional skill, engaging in a challenging new experience, switching focus onto a different area of endeavor, or extracting yourself from a well-worn rut)?

Imagine how you'll feel if you reach your target. Try visualizing and actively identifying with the more energized, productive, healthy, fulfilled, connected, creative, repotted version of your current self. How wonderful you'll feel when you're running up and down those stairs without all that unattractive panting. Imagine the weight lifted from your shoulders once you've put your personal finances in order. And think about how optimistic and confident you'll feel once that qualification has been added to your name.

Is your repotting project designed to help or benefit others? If so, who or what? Try thinking about how other people's lives would improve if your efforts were successful. Visualize them leading healthier, better educated, better housed, more empowered, or less lonely lives. If your project involves a cause or a movement, imagine what might happen if that issue were better understood, better funded, or more widely embraced.

What are your personal repotting objectives?

Make these clear, concise, achievable, and measurable. For example: study for 3 hours a day, 3 days a week for 6 months to acquire my target qualification; shed 2 pounds a week for x

weeks, lose *y*, and reach my target weight of *z*; try to remember enough math to work out what I mean by *x*, *y*, and *z*.

What's the time frame?

Does your repotting plan involve an incremental implementation process that might require many months or years? If so, what are the critical milestones within these phases? To help get you started, can you create a schedule for any tasks that you need to accomplish in the short term?

What help might you need along the way?

Do you need to team up with partners or organizations who can offer you complementary strengths or support? If so, what experience, expertise, credibility, funding, or other benefits do you require from them? Do you know of people who have already trodden a similar path to the one you're thinking of taking? Is there any way you can reach out and connect with them either through friends, colleagues, or like-minded communities or support groups?

How can you manage the risks of uprooting?

There's nothing you can do to anticipate or manage every single potential risk. Risk is a normal part of everyday life, but with preparation, you'll feel more confident in dealing with whatever curveball life decides to throw. Life is full of risks even if you decide to stay stuck in the same old miserable rut, so you may as well plan, take the plunge, and have a go at better things.

Aside from preparation and planning, another way to manage your natural anxiety is to give yourself the emotional counterbalance of hope. If you can paint a clear mental picture, the more detailed the better, of your potential new future, then you're more likely to remain attracted toward this positive vision and feel inspired to get moving. You might, for example, draw up a list of all the negatives associated with the situation that you're trying to leave behind and, at the same time, compile a list of all the positives you're now trying to achieve. As seasoning for your own "feel the fear and do it anyway" recipe, you might find it helpful to add generous dollops of intense emotion. Fear, shame, embarrassment, panic, weariness, anger, and outrage might be elements featuring on your negative list, while joy, excitement, love, enthusiasm, and euphoria might be among the positive ones. These intense feelings will help "fix" the initial motivation for your plans to uproot more firmly in your mind and encourage you to keep going when times get tough.

Susannah Constantine, a well-known and highly successful British media personality, has written poignantly about her struggle to uproot from her potbound pattern of alcoholism. In an open letter designed to help others extricating themselves from the same predicament, she speaks movingly of feeling demotivated, directionless, and depressed and of trying to numb these classic, telltale potbound signs with increasing quantities of booze. Added to this, children becoming more independent and a parent nearing the end of her life heralded a period of disquieting change that further exacerbated her feelings of discomfort. Although she clearly managed to hide the situation well, she gradually found that this potbound existence was making her feel isolated and the effort involved in not extracting herself left her totally exhausted. Despite feelings of shame and guilt, however, it was only when she blacked out, fell, and fractured various bones in her back, resulting in physical agony, that the emotional impetus was strong enough to make her change direction and repot for a healthier life.

This example may sound extreme, but it serves to illustrate the power of intense emotional reactions to a dark and difficult situation. If you're still concerned about moving on, try the following exercise:

1. Paint a picture of all the positives you hope to achieve by your particular repotting. If you think about the testimony above, for example, that might include: waking up in the morning and feeling enthusiastic about starting the day; remembering clearly what you said to various people yesterday and feeling happy about your social interactions with others; going to bed at night with a clear head and feeling liberated, energized, free, from guilt, and eager to engage in tomorrow's life-enhancing activities.

2. Paint the grimmest picture of all the negatives from which you are trying to extract yourself. Working on the same kind of example, you might recall, for instance: the exploding skull and cement-mixer stomach associated with your last stratospheric humdinger of a hangover; the toe-curling guilt when reminded of your impromptu pole-dancing routine at the office party; the stay-buried-under-the-duvet shame of coming around to find yourself somewhere you really oughtn't to be.

3. Keep working on the pictures until the positives outweigh the negatives. It may take some time, various iterations, and a few failed attempts, but the moment the positives tip the scales, you'll know you're ready to uproot.

Although I am not advocating the degree of obsessive planning that leads to "planstipation" and its consequent lack of action, there's no doubt that the best way to keep your fear under control is to flesh out your plan with just enough detail to mitigate your natural anxieties. Let's have a look at a few other possible obstacles and do a further breakdown of what uprooting might involve for you. Let's establish how—with the right preparation—this often very demanding process of transition can be managed with more ease.

Eliminate pests

For several years running, on the basis that I had written a couple of books about sports that had somehow ended up on the *Sunday Times* bestsellers list, I was invited to join the judging panel for the UK's William Hill Sports Book of the Year award. Too often, the memoirs of sporting celebrities come as a terrific disappointment—hastily ghostwritten confections of cliché, claptrap, and score-settling of breathtaking banality. It therefore always fills me with great joy when I come across a book by an outstanding sportsman whose reflections on the page match his talent on the field. One such book was *Addicted* by soccer player Tony Adams, published in 1999 and written when its protagonist was still captain of Arsenal and England and less than three years after he had revealed his own very different story of alcohol addiction and the tough, often lonely, battle he had to wage in order to clean up his act. Reading this strikingly honest book, you were left wondering not only how Adams could have maintained his performance at the highest level, but how he even managed to get himself onto the soccer field at all. I still recall one of the key insights he shared about trying desperately to break away from his old lifestyle. In order to redirect himself along the right path, Adams gradually found himself forced to drop the company of old drinking buddies and the comforting familiarity of many of their favored old haunts.

It may seem heartless, but like all good gardeners, you have to realize that pests must be eradicated if you intend to maintain a healthy environment that allows you to thrive. Pests can include anyone in your life who drains, weakens, confuses, or distracts you instead of supporting and encouraging. You've all met the human equivalent of the Asian hornet, a vicious creature capable of destroying entire communities of productive and useful honeybees. Or those endlessly needy "friends" who are more like aphids that attach their sucking mouthparts to the veins of leaves and drain the lifeblood from a healthy tree. A great friend of mine was once involved with a man whom we all dubbed

Convolvulus after the weak-stemmed, prostrate, and invasive weed that surreptitiously insinuates itself around vigorous plants and ends up strangling them. Like *Convolvulus*, this character ended up bleeding her dry before slithering on to attach himself to the next unwary victim.

Letting go of some of your existing, less helpful connections can be particularly tough because the people most invested in wanting you to stay the same are often those you know best or with whom you are most closely involved. Perhaps most problematic, however, are those people whose intense emotional dependence is often conflated with love. Whether it's the clinging mama resisting her son's attempts to snip the apron strings, or the disruptive behavior of the grown-up child determined to stop his divorced parent from dating again, there will always be those around us with their own unresolved reasons for trying to strangle our growth. Ending these unhelpful relationships entirely or spelling out the nonnegotiable nature of your plans for repotting can be a real challenge. How, then, can you mark out clear borders, reclaim boundaries that have already been overstepped, and ward off the pests that are continually trying to encroach? Whereas casual relationships are relatively easy to deal with (we can all imagine inserting the Apple AirPods, pulling down the eye mask, and simulating snoring when the loquacious looney next to us on a flight shows signs of lathering on all the way from London to Los Angeles), our more important personal and professional relationships need to be managed more diplomatically. The following pest-control exercise may help:

1. Is there a person you can confide in who might help you reset the boundaries with someone who has overstepped the mark and is making what you feel are unreasonable demands on you?

2. Can you rely on this person's personal and/or professional discretion?

3. If you're dealing with an especially tricky family member, is there an ally who can advise or help you confront them without unleashing a fully fledged family feud?

4. Although some in your inner circle will support and encourage you in your repotting process, others will feel alarmed by the prospect of change. Bait the hook to suit the fish! If genuine stakeholders in your life feel threatened by your prospective repotting, try explaining that your decision is made *for* you and not in any way *against* them. People who genuinely have your best interests at heart will understand. The others cannot be allowed to hold you back.

5. There may be individuals whose influence is so negative that they are best eradicated from your life entirely. Can you identify such individuals in your life? Are they inalienably or exclusively associated with situations, behaviors, or patterns that you are now trying to leave behind? Are you prepared to let these people go? If so, how can you ensure that the separation is on your terms and with as little damage as possible to you?

6. If you do have pests in your life, can you explain how they managed to worm their way in there in the first place? Are you prepared to man your own barricades, stand on your own two feet, and rely on your own resources in order to protect yourself against such unwelcome intrusions and distractions in the future?

Like many of you, prior to my most recent repotting iteration, I had already undergone various repottings, some more radical than others. In my experience, a few key people will remain forever in my life and, thanks to my most recent experience, I've been lucky enough to add a few more to that core group. These are people whose mutual support and affection is unconditional and who neither demand nor expect anything else from each other. Whenever I've moved on, however, there's always been a natural culling of outer-circle people whose interests may no longer coincide with mine but whose company I've enjoyed in the past and with whom I'd happily reconnect if our paths ever crossed again. And then there's the pests—the energy thieves who creep into your life whenever you fail to value yourself, your time, and your efforts. It happens to us all, but once you focus on implementing your own rigorous repotting plan, you'll soon find that you have no spare resources left over for the pests to draw on and you'll have de facto eradicated them from your life.

Prune and deadhead

Avid gardeners will be familiar with the 3 Ds of pruning: Anything that is dead, diseased, or damaged should be pruned away as soon as possible without waiting for a specific season. The same is true for repotters. When you are moving from one stage of life to another, you need to get rid of anything that deflects, distracts, or in any way delays your progress.

Perhaps it's because I live in a Victorian house surrounded by antique shops that I'm fascinated by the Victorians' mania for "stuff" and the degree of domestic (for domestic, read historically *women's*) servitude that this accumulation of clutter invariably demanded. Instead of battling for emancipation or working for their PhDs in science, technology, engineering, and math, for instance, many nineteenth-century women were kept busy with such monumental concerns as ensuring that the backs of their chairs and sofas were covered with antimacassars—those pieces of linen designed to protect the upholstery from their menfolk's Macassar hair oil—which had to be laundered daily. Can you imagine a more egregious waste of anyone's time and energy? The whole host of tyrannical trifles that bound generations of women to the hearth of genteel underachievement! Of course, it's easy to poke fun at buttoned-down and starched-up Victorian behavior, but the truth is that modern, consumer-based capitalism has encouraged us to acquire even more "stuff" than ever before. I recognize that there's something very comforting about being surrounded by your "stuff," but an excess of "stuff," however desirable, valuable, and collectible, can easily end up enslaving us. How often have you struggled with a caravan of everything-but-the-kitchen-sink-bulging suitcases while enviously eyeing those fellow airport travelers who've Marie Kondoed their entire week's requirements into a "hand baggage only" solution?

Having excess-baggaged myself for far too long, I am now a firm believer that "stuff" simply slows you down. It deflects your attention away from the things that really matter and clutters up the road to your new repotted existence. In my own case, given that my repotting process involved relocating from one country to another, the process of jettisoning many material possessions was also an immensely practical imperative. For months before heading off to California, I heaved countless bags of virtually unworn clothes to the local charity shops. The consequences were unexpected—not least because for weeks before my departure from London the neighborhood was populated with a disturbing invasion of Frances Edmonds doppelgängers—every one a distinctly enhanced version of the increasingly pruned original. And, paradoxically, with all the clutter removed from my comprehensively culled closet, there seemed to be far more options now hanging there that I actually wanted to wear.

A far harder sacrifice involved letting go of the majority of my lifetime's collection of books, only marginally mitigated by the knowledge that the world's library was still readily available on my Kindle and iPad. Then went the excess furniture, including the piano that I'd never found time to master, after which all my remaining possessions were dispatched into storage. And finally, when all that was done and dusted, I put my beloved home of thirty years up for rent.

The purge, however, continued. An inveterate news junkie, I weaned myself off listening to the vast majority of current affairs programs. Dominated during that period by Brexit, the UK news seemed to have degenerated into a grindingly repetitive loop that highlighted the dystopia of a 24/7 news cycle. Vox pop interviews with average Joes spouting drivel were spliced with so-called expert commentary from talking heads delivering the same old arguments—the whole dreary and debilitating media circus served up in place of any genuinely newsworthy developments. None of this bouillabaisse of bullshit was adding much to the sum total of my understanding and, if truth be told, the whole sorry saga was starting to depress me. As a British citizen who'd spent much of her professional life working for EU organizations, I felt viscerally conflicted, angry at the theatrical grandstanding being played out in both the UK and the EU. Eventually, the wisdom encapsulated in the Serenity Prayer kicked in: When there's nothing that you personally can do to change a situation, then back off and devote your energy to those things you can. Having broken free from the shackles of rolling news coverage by the simple expedient of confining myself to a daily digest, I felt encouraged to embark on an even more radical pruning rampage. Never a heavy user of social media, I've always avoided the systemically splenetic sections of those platforms where confected and technology-enhanced outrage compete to distort and displace informed discourse. Nevertheless, I cut back even further. Screen time once devoted to giving two hoots about other people's kids, cats, and culinary proclivities was more fruitfully redirected into hacking through the avalanche of administration required for my next move. I read somewhere that global average social media usage is around two and a half hours a day—which meant there were probably one hundred and fifty waking minutes I could be more usefully spending on my own stuff. I logged out of social media apps, which then involved going through the hassle of logging in again whenever I wanted to access them. Even this minor obstacle resulted in making me stop and think, and in a more moderate and mindful use of my phone.

I was on a roll. The more outworn things and activities I junked, the more energized I felt to continue the process. Soon I began to feel the psychological as well as the physical and mental benefits of pruning: a growing sense of liberation, a lightness of spirit, and an untrammeled excitement about the possibilities of the future. Not only was it motivating, but there was something nonnegotiable about the shedding process too—it felt like a kind of scorched-earth policy, removing all of the fallback options that might have allowed me to turn back. Not only had I burned my bridges, I'd bombed my bunker, blasted my belongings, and blown up the backstop of any possible Plan B. I was pulling up each and every one of my firmly embedded roots in order to give them a different, more propitious space to flourish. It's clear that not every repotting journey will involve a dramatic upheaval, a new country, or a complete change of direction, and your own pre-repotting purge might focus on issues other than your physical possessions or your time-honored habits. In any event, however, you may find it helpful to consider which aspects of your current life are taking up unnecessary or wasteful amounts of your time and energy:

1. People and activities generally fall into two categories: *Radiators* generate energy and positivity, whereas *drains* (see also pests above) suck your vitality from you and leave you feeling exhausted. Identify the radiators and drains in your life. If drains have legitimate calls on your time and energy, they must somehow be factored into your life; if they have no such claims, reduce the time and energy you spend with or on them.

2. Beware of any silent-killer requests involving the words *just* and *only*, as in "You wouldn't mind *just* . . ." or "It'll *only* take . . ." You can't really imagine Mozart managing to compose his sublime body of music if Mrs. Mozart was forever interrupting his creative flow with, "Oy, Wolfgang, you wouldn't mind just slipping out to the shop for a few sausages for supper, would you? It'll only take a few minutes." Instead of instantly

agreeing to accommodate every request that comes your way, try occasionally adopting the "I'll get back to you on that one" technique. In this way, you give yourself the opportunity to mull over the time and headspace of what's involved. You can then make an informed decision on whether you want to play ball or not.

3. As Aristotle famously observed, a friend to all is a friend to none. If you constantly give too much of yourself to others, you end up losing yourself and your sense of direction. Once you've identified the pests and drains in your life, learn the *art of saying no*. Sometimes "No" is the only right answer when you need to clear the headspace required to move on with your repotting plan.

4. Eliminate as many decisions as possible. Most of us tend to be bad decision-makers and waste hundreds of hours making insignificant or even redundant choices every year. With planning, you can prune away a lot of your time-wasting decisions. You can, for example, prepare your work outfit, your meals, or your to-do list before going to bed. Not only will you probably sleep better with all those preying concerns now off your mind, but you'll also avoid wasting precious mental energy on insignificant decisions the next morning.

5. Edit your to-do list. Most of us have a tendency to try to get far more done than is possible in the time available. We compile infinite to-do lists and then end up feeling stressed when we can't complete them. Now is the time to prune! There are probably items on that list that can easily be deleted without leaving anything important undone. You don't have to knock yourself out being manically busy all the time—just prioritize according to importance and urgency and then proceed at your own speed.

6. Eliminate impulse purchases. If your repotting involves getting on top of your personal finances, you have only two realistic options: Increase your income and/or decrease your expenses. In the vast majority of cases, and I have some experience here, the most useless purchases occur when you buy something without thinking much about it. Next time you see something you don't need but you'd like to buy, wait for at least twenty-four hours before getting it. This will help you avoid emotionally driven purchases and decide whether you *really* want that item.

These and similar minor pruning exercises may seem unimportant at first, but over the years they will yield extraordinary benefits in terms of the time, money, and energy saved that can be directed to your own successful repotting.

Create the right headspace

Tackling all the hurdles listed above is tough to begin with, but once you get into your stride, you'll begin to feel more confident and assertive. As you create and develop your own headspace, you become more acutely mindful of other people's boundaries, which, in turn, inhibits you from inappropriate meddling in their affairs and further clears the way for you to progress along your own repotting path. We could all do with learning to recognize when justifiable concern slips into unwarranted intrusion and when well-meant help morphs into gratuitous interference. So how might you draw the right boundaries to demarcate your turf and simultaneously free up the headspace that you need to uproot and move on?

Your turf covers everything from your experiences to your personal growth and professional development; from your mistakes to your physical, intellectual, emotional, and spiritual well-being; from your happiness and the quality of your relationships to your personal environment; and from your addictions and habits to your financial security. All these matters are *your* responsibility.

Remember that *beyond* your boundaries lies other people's turf. Accept that *their* turf is *their* responsibility and how they choose to live and experience their lives is therefore entirely up to *them*. It is not your responsibility to offer advice unless it's requested or unless you've been granted permission to give it. It is not your responsibility to involve yourself in whether or how those individuals decide to implement or disregard your advice.

Once you reach a clear understanding of what is and is not your legitimate responsibility, your own path becomes much clearer. Many people find that solutions including meditation, mindfulness, or MBSR (mindfulness-based stress reduction) are helpful in pruning distractions and training attention. These are powerful techniques but can take time, often a lifetime, to master effectively.

I recently came across a simple regime that anyone can deploy with more immediate effect and that helps you uproot and move on from the past by focusing on quick wins in the near future. Start by writing down three things that you want to achieve within the next twelve months, for example, getting fit, learning a language, and sorting out your finances. Every day thereafter, commit to doing one thing that helps toward achieving each of those goals. If you're trying to master a language, for example, download any one of the many language apps on offer nowadays and learn a few new words every day. If you want to sort out your finances, begin by finding yourself a good bookkeeper or accountant or, if you think you can manage by yourself, sign up for an online financial literacy course. And if you're trying to get fit and don't want to kick off by working out with the six-pack peacocks down at the gym, why not start by taking a brisk daily walk—ideally not straight to the pub.

Identify what other support you're going to need

One reason that uprooting can feel stressful is because we are forced to recognize that it may require resources that we fear we don't possess. The best way to start managing this particular fear is to consider all the resources that you *have* managed to acquire over the years. At this point, you might find it useful to refer back to the list of personal strengths, achievements, talents, transferable skills, etc. that you compiled in chapter 2. Now that you've established what your next repotting move might involve and given yourself the headspace to create the plan required to make it happen, it's time to figure out what's still missing in terms of skills, advice, and resources. Obviously, you'll never be able to anticipate everything that will come up, but it's always useful to write down a list of the questions that you need answered and identify who to ask.

To take my own example, I was renting out my house in London and moving to California to take up a fellowship at Stanford. Quite apart from the reading, research, and all-around improvement in IT skills that I needed to address before my departure, I realized that I also needed to create an administrative checklist that would make my uprooting process as painless as possible, if acquiring a US J1 visa can in any way be considered painless. When the repotting involved is complex, working your way through a roadmap helps you feel that you're making progress, if only by covering short legs of the journey every single day. An expurgated, bowdlerized, and heavily edited version of my roadmap (there were days when some of my additional comments might have broken the rules of decency) looked something like this:

In the UK

1. Rent out house. Call friends in EuRA (European Relocation Association) to advise on good managing agent.

2. Managing agent to advise on best local real estate agent re: renting. Advice on health and safety/utilities certificates required to rent out house. Ask agent what else I need to do.

3. Organize furniture/contents removal/storage (contact in relocation business).

4. Organize relevant house insurance (contact in relocation business).

5. Organize redirection of mail (post office website).

6. Create relevant standing orders (online banking).

7. Store car outside of London.

For the USA

1. J1 visa. (US government website plus documentation required from Stanford plus interview at US Embassy in London plus detailed record of my every arrival and departure to/from USA going back to the Boston Tea Party.)

2. Rent apartment in Palo Alto. (Advice from British friends already at Stanford.)

3. Furniture, etc. for apartment. (Ask UK relocation friends for US contact and advice.)

4. Health insurance for USA. (Nightmare! Advice from British friends at Stanford.)

5. Open US bank account. (Complicated. Seems US banks need a US address before they'll give me a bank account. Seems US real estate agents need me to have a US bank account before they'll allow me to sign a lease! Ask Alexandra [my daughter, already in US] to act as my guarantor? LOL!)

6. WiFi, US cell phone, etc. (Advice from US relocation contact/British friends at Stanford.)

7. Getting around in US. Buy a car? (Website on driving in California. Requirement to pass written and road tests for Californian driver's license. Seems like too much hassle right now. Buy a bike? Walk more! Get fit!)

Such lists, by their nature, are boring and banal, and many items that look simple on paper end up being unexpectedly and horribly complex. None of that really matters! Even if a single item on your list (e.g., US visa or rent apartment) spawns multiple further items, the point of this exercise is that it sets you off in the right direction on a series of small, incremental steps. Each one of these steps demands your attention, increases your feeling of control, and thereby encourages you to feel more comfortable about uprooting. The process of systematically working your way through the challenges posed by your future plan and resolutely checking off each and every item listed is both energizing and motivational. Believe me, once you've successfully negotiated an American visa, you feel ready to take on the world.

Build a support network

As my own list above clearly demonstrates, once you have some idea of what it is that you need to know, it's time to start reaching out to the people who might have the answers. Although you can discover the solutions to many of your questions on the internet or in a book, the key to successful repotting resides in building and harnessing a network of people who, for whatever reason, feel inclined to lend a hand and help when you ask. Some of these people will be on the list of resources that you compiled when creating your headspace. Others will be names unearthed as you identified the support you were going to need. But there will also be plenty of others that you don't expect. One of my literary touchstones is Dante's *Divine Comedy*. It is the metaphorical story of the author himself—Dante—who is "*nel mezzo del cammin*" or "midway in the journey" of his life and finds himself lost in a dark wood. Trying desperately to get himself back on the right track, he searches for guidance and gains unexpected allies in the form of the Roman poet Virgil and the unattainable object of his own devotion, Beatrice, who help him navigate his way through Hell, Purgatory, and on toward Paradise. I've often thought that the misery of feeling potbound might be considered the secular equivalent to Hell; that the pain of learning from past mistakes, uprooting, and attempting to move on may often be experienced as Purgatory; and that the rewards of personal renewal earned at the end of every success-ful repotting journey might well be regarded as earthly Paradise. And just like Dante, however lost and anxious you may feel, once you recognize your predicament and seek help to move on, it's surprising how allies appear to support you.

It's curious how you may even find that some of these allies have been around for ages but, somehow, you've never noticed them because they weren't of interest or relevance to you until now. I can still recall London's boiling summer in 1989 when I was heavily pregnant. As I went about my business looking like an ostrich with two incongruously scrawny legs protruding from a bulbously ballooning body, it seemed to me that half of London was also about to give birth. Could it possibly have been that there was a sudden population explosion in London that particular summer? Or was the simple explanation that I was paying more attention to people and phenomena that had suddenly become relevant to me? As soon as you are on the lookout for allies, you'll find they crop up all over the place.

The trick to finding the support you need is to become a master in the art of networking. This doesn't mean that you have to become one of those ghastly look-over-the-shoulder-of-the-person-you're-talking-to-and-see-if-there's-anyone-else-more-important-in-the-room hustlers. Nor does it mean making every conversation revolve around you and your needs. If you want to avoid becoming one of those people who gives networking a bad name, just remember the following golden rules:

1. Open your mind. The best networkers never assume who will or won't be interesting or helpful; they are genuinely curious about other people and open to diverse perspectives, ideas, and experiences. I'm often asked why I've spent a vast part of my lifetime learning foreign languages "when everyone speaks English." My answer to that old chestnut is that it's for exactly the same reason that I prefer to watch television in color and not in black and white. Diversity adds a deeper texture to everyday life, and networkers who delight in connecting across multiple languages, nationalities, disciplines, industries, socioeconomic groupings, situations, functions, and ages

will not only be the most effective but they'll also be experiencing life with infinitely more vibrant intensity. So, with that in mind, always be ready to strike up a conversation with the people you encounter, especially when they too have changed the way they work and live. It's easy. Just ask them a question and don't persist if they don the eye mask and insert the AirPods.

2. Be generous. Aggressively self-interested and transactional networkers may make progress initially, but they'll get only so far before word of their self-centered attitude gets out and the communal well of goodwill runs dry. The most generous and effective networker I've ever met combines a high-powered, public company board-level position with pro bono work both for an international charity and the local high school while still finding time to help just about every person who ever crosses her path. I have no idea how she manages to "do it all," but her boundless energy seems to stem from the satisfaction she derives from consistently helping and connecting other people. For her, networking is not a professional add-on but a life skill, one that she employs with respect, care, and indomitable joie de vivre irrespective of the challenges she's dealing with in her personal life. When you approach relationship-building and networking

with this spirit of generosity, you'll find that all sorts of other people respond to you in like manner. You'll end up learning from unexpected sources and you'll remain open to benefitting from new experiences as you make your way along the right path.

3. Reach out. By all means enlist the support of close family, friends, and colleagues to help you with your repotting journey, but don't stop there. In his pioneering paper "The Strength of Weak Ties," Stanford sociologist Mark Granovetter explains how your inner circle can be of only so much help—firstly, because they probably have much the same information and perspective as you, and secondly, because they know you and categorize you according to your current status and situation. They therefore find it harder to think of you in a new way. It's far better, says Granovetter, to make use of your "weak ties," including those casual acquaintances and friends of friends who can provide you with new information, introduce you to new networks, and whose advice is not limited by any preexisting ideas about you.

4. Overcome any feelings of awkwardness. Harnessing the potential of your weak ties can sometimes feel awkward. If you're contacting the friend of a friend, the best thing to do is to be polite, mention your mutual acquaintance,

be straight about why you're getting in touch, and make it clear that any help would be appreciated. Then, if you haven't heard anything after a suitable juncture, you can follow up with a second message asking them if they have had time to think about it. What can potentially feel more uncomfortable is contacting people whom you used to know but have lost touch with, such as old school friends or work colleagues. Unless you were the mean girl at school who made this long-lost contact's life a misery, or the groom who now wants to access the woman you once left standing in tears at the altar, ask yourself what's the worst that can happen. When you get in touch, just acknowledge the years of silence and then get to the point. Explain why you're getting in touch and allow the other person off the hook with a ready-made get-out ("I realize that you're probably rushed off your feet . . ."). Maybe they'll ignore you, but ask yourself what you would do if you found yourself in the same circumstances. The chances are that you'd happily lend a hand. You might even be delighted to renew the friendship. So why would they feel any differently?

5. Be specific. As someone who has done a lot of public speaking and who has coached various clients to do the same, I can tell you that the key is to connect swiftly with

your audience. Most people called on to speak publicly usually know their subject inside out. They've even usually worked out the message that they want to convey. Far too often, however, they fail to talk in terms that engage the audience's interest. When you reach out to people for support, don't bore them to death with the unexpurgated version of your cry-me-a-river drama. Just cut to the chase. I suggest you formulate your approach along "What? So what? Now what?" lines. Explain briefly what it is that you want. If possible, explain why the person you are talking to might want to listen or help (e.g., a shared contact, mutual friend, or a common interest in a subject). Be specific about your request. What precisely do you want this person to do? (Not so much of the vague "I'm thinking of moving to the USA" routine—more of the "Do you know any good real estate agents in Palo Alto?" approach.)

Think of others

Whatever the circumstances of your uprooting, unless you're currently living as a hermit, your forthcoming decision to separate yourself in some way from a particular phase in your life will inevitably impact on others. I know of a man, for example, who ended his long-standing marriage with a fax message (clinical and callous); another who never bothered to inform any one of his succession of wives when he had effectively left and moved on to the next (covert and cowardly); and yet another who left his children eagerly waiting for him at home, never to return (covert, cowardly, and callous).

On the whole, uprooting is not best managed under the cloud cover of cowardice or against a backdrop of carnage. Repotters should not behave like quitters or bolters or complete and utter bastards. Those people in your world who have a legitimate interest in your decisions should be treated with consideration and, in most personal situations, with empathy and kindness. They certainly don't deserve to wake up one morning to find that you've headed off on a sudden solo around-the-world yacht trip in search of your inner child. It's not a question of your prevaricating; it's more that everyone involved needs the appropriate time to assimilate your reasoned and reasonable decision.

If partners, children, family, or colleagues are going to be affected by your need to uproot, you may have to create temporary structures and arrangements while you all work your way through the emotional upheaval and practical considerations of your decision. If you are leaving a job with a good employer, for instance, you may feel inclined to help recruit your replacement. If you are leaving a relationship, you may need to make the appropriate housing or childcare arrangements to accommodate everyone involved.

My own uprooting was fraught with anxiety and distress at the thought of having to say goodbye to my increasingly frail mother who was, at that stage, in her late nineties and in failing health. One word from her and I would have called the whole project off but, consistent with the selfless woman she had been all her life, she encouraged me to set sail with her blessing. I was also fortunate in having three wonderfully supportive medical brothers and partners living in close proximity to her. Whatever happened in my absence, I knew that she would be in the best of hands and that we had parted leaving nothing between us unsaid.

At the other end of the generational spectrum, I was also concerned about my daughter, Alexandra, and her reaction to the idea of Mummy Edmonds turning up and spoiling her fun at Stanford, the place to which she herself had recently repotted. This conversation proved rather more tricky and, as might be expected from a Stanford MBA student, she laid out very clear protocols, regulations, and territorial boundaries on agreement of which, and subject to any changes in terms and conditions she might unilaterally deem necessary, I was granted a license to operate.

Decision time

A great friend of mine used to train the UK's Royal Marine commandos—the crack troops celebrated for their meticulously planned, hyperefficient handling of the toughest situations. When discussing their success, he used to talk about three key stages: Information—Decision—Execution.

1. Information. Identify the situation that needs to be handled. Gather as much information as possible on it. Assess that information. Set a goal.

2. Decision. Formulate a plan. Communicate it to whoever needs to know. Give the order.

3. Execution. No questions. No looking back. Commit to the plan. As my military friend used to sign off on all his emails, "On! On!"

Over the course of these first three chapters, we have identified the need for action, defined the kind of action required, armed ourselves with as much information as we can, and communicated our plan of action to everyone who needs to know.

The next step is in many senses the most dramatic one: giving yourself the order to go for it. For many would-be repotters, this is where all the negative thoughts that have contributed to your previous potbound predicament will converge to create one of life's genuine make-or-break moments. This is when you start asking yourself whether you're really going to go for it. Maybe you'd be better going for it tomorrow instead, or next month might be better, or perhaps next year? Or maybe you need a little bit more information before you finally commit? What if you're missing out by not waiting for a better option? And perhaps the dog needs to go for a walk.

This procrastinating routine can go on forever if you allow it to. In the end, it's up to you to decide to take the plunge. For some people, the telltale sign will be an unmistakable gut feeling that it's now or never. For others, the following external prompts may prove helpful:

1. Give yourself a specific date as a deadline. The reason that negotiations have deadlines is precisely to focus minds and avoid potentially endless discussions.

2. Decide on an event, or confluence of events, that will signal decision-making time for you: if I don't get a promotion this time around, I'm looking for another job; if he breaks his promise to stop gambling one more time, I'm out of here; if I'm offered a place in the program, I'll definitely go.

3. Commit to your plan in public or, even better, make a solemn promise to yourself that you'll do it.

4. Just do it!

Pull up the roots

"Whatever you can do or dream you can, begin," advised German writer and statesman Johann Wolfgang von Goethe. "Boldness has genius, power, and magic in it." There are few forces in nature more powerfully motivating than the energy to break free from the shackles of stasis and start. Occasionally, friends with an idea for a book will ask me about the so-called book-writing process. They fondly imagine hours spent communing with the Muses or perhaps plucking inspiration from passing clouds. They invariably look disappointed when I tell them that my own technique is rather less glamorous and that all you can do is commit. I then explain that commitment rarely involves clouds or Muses of any description, but rather sitting alone every day for what seems like an eternity, staring desperately at a blank page until your brain bleeds, and doggedly putting down one word after another. That usually puts them off, and who knows how many brilliant books never got off the ground for lack of commitment to that chair–backside requirement?

So what does committing to repot look like? Let's take an example. Say you decide that you want to repot and make yourself financially secure. From where you currently are, that may feel like a massive mountain to climb. To get yourself going, you need a gadfly to prod you into action. Why not challenge yourself to commit to something relatively simple at first, like deciding to stop those impulse purchases and pay off your credit cards every month.

Or say that you decide you want to work toward something more ephemeral, like feeling happy and fulfilled—another daunting Everest of an aspiration. In this instance, you'll probably find it more productive to think in comparative as opposed to absolute terms. Ask yourself a different question to get yourself moving. Instead of wondering what would make you happy and fulfilled, ask instead what small step would make you feel even marginally *more* happy and *more* fulfilled. The answer might be something as modest as taking a daily stroll or watching the birds in your garden, but the point is that you're off the starting block and you're already on your way.

In my case, commitment involved the simple act of sending in my application to Stanford. I knew I couldn't control the outcome, but that action in itself represented my irreversible decision to move on to a new phase in my life. The process of transformation that followed began with the mere click of a mouse.

You have looked objectively at your present pot, identified how uncomfortable it is and how it limits your possibilities for growth and satisfaction. You have a vision of what your life might be like once free of all those restrictions, when the changes you are preparing to make will allow your roots to stretch and extend further into rich new soil, refreshing you and refueling you for the future. Now the time has come to make that vision a reality. How inviting that expansive new pot and its reenergizing contents look. The details of how you're going to fit in aren't necessarily clear yet, but you have made the decision to get going. Bon voyage!

SUMMARY

1. It is normal to find the repotting process uncomfortable. Hold on to a positive vision of your future and find focus and reassurance in working through the details of your plan.

2. Purge your life of all the people, possessions, and behaviors that are sapping your energy or holding you back.

3. Clear the headspace you require to think and plan your next move.

4. Audit the resources you already have that will help you reach your repotting destination. Identify the resources that you don't yet have and consider how you are going to acquire or access them.

5. Assemble a support network, following the golden rules of networking.

6. Inform everyone who will be affected by your decision. Negotiate ways to minimize any negative consequences of your decision on their lives.

7. Follow the Commando's Code: Information—Decision—Execution.

8. Pull up your roots. It's time to repot.

BEDDING IN

What sort of adjustments will be necessary once you start life in your new pot? What challenges will you face and how can you overcome them?

After waiting for three hours or so to be checked by US Customs and Border Protection, any "yearning to breathe free" I might have been experiencing—as the welcoming verse on the nation's Statue of Liberty suggests—was waging an increasingly desperate battle against losing the will to live. Surely San Francisco's airport, the gateway to Silicon Valley, the world's undisputed leader in advanced technology, ought to be more efficient than this? In the line, where a misspelling or a mistaken date in paperwork might lead to instant refusal of entry, people shuffled slowly in submissive silence, pallid at the thought of a typing error. There was something about the whole process that made you feel unaccountably guilty for crimes you've never even imagined in your wildest psychopathic dreams. Despite my cheeks suffused with a felony-suggesting flush, the lemon-lipped lady who triple-checked my documentation was minded to accept my denials of mass murder, terrorism, and Class A drug-dealing. At last I was at liberty to enter the Land of the Free.

It hadn't been easy to stuff a sixty-odd-year life into a single suitcase, but thanks to my belatedly discovered decluttering discipline, I'd arrived to spend an entire year in the USA with less baggage than I'd normally pack for a long weekend in Paris. Increasingly, I could feel the benefits of systematic shedding and, if I wasn't exactly soaring like an eagle or gliding like a swan, at least I wasn't reenacting my usual routine of plodding like a packhorse. It was therefore with the smug sigh of the vindicated shedder that I slumped into the back seat of my Uber ride, ready to brave the early-evening rush hour on State Route 82. For the first time since I'd learned how to drive way back in the early seventies, I'd decided not to get bogged down in the business of owning my own car in the USA. Not only had the break-the-camel's-back administrative hassle of acquiring a Californian driver's license put me off, but it felt as if all the simplification I'd sought to achieve in uprooting would be undermined if I went and saddled myself with another set of four wheels. Setting up the Uber app on my phone before I left London, I'd felt proud at my own resourcefulness and open-minded determination to adapt to the Brave New World of the sharing economy. It was only when calls started coming in from irritated strangers at unknown numbers that I realized I'd somehow managed to hook myself up to the system as an Uber driver as opposed to an Uber client. Platforms, I soon realized, are all very well so long as you're on the right one.

My first ride as an Uber passenger progressed without a hitch, although, it must be admitted, with a very definite whiff of something akin to cannabis wafting around inside the vehicle. Forty minutes later, and slightly glassy-eyed, I found myself deposited outside an apartment block in Palo Alto, the modest town that serves Stanford University and the adjacent Silicon Valley community. Heading up to my new home on the twelfth floor of the block and by now a bit befuddled by my long flight and the vicarious vaping afforded by my ride, it wasn't long before I crawled into bed and conked out into a deep sleep.

A few hours later, in the dead of night, I found myself being jolted awake by the unmistakable tremor of an earthquake. I was well aware, of course, that Palo Alto is what Californians call "seismically challenged" and that the area is subject to the occasional tectonic tantrums of the San Andreas Fault. I also knew that my building— like all recent constructions—had been designed with suitable earthquake-proofing provisions. This assurance afforded little solace, however, as I sat bolt upright in bed contemplating my precarious position twelve stories above the shaking ground. Time for a swift reframe. How fortunate I was to have my few possessions still compacted into a single suitcase! Wondering frantically whether I was supposed to head for the hills or seek refuge under the bed, I fumbled for my phone, where a local news feed informed me that this was "only" a 4.4 magnitude tremor and that I was advised to stay exactly where I was. I snuggled back under the duvet satisfied that in some strange, symbolic sense, I had made it safely to the other side. I'd made my move and now I'd sunk my roots into new—if shifting—soil.

LOOK FOR THE POSITIVES

Doubt and anxiety come with the territory when it comes to repotting, and you'll frequently find yourself oscillating and having to choose between your old potbound pessimism and your newfound repotter optimism. There's a glorious story, sadly apocryphal, about two identical twins celebrating their joint birthday. The first twin wakes up to find the corner of his bedroom stacked with expensive presents: the latest four-prop quadcopter drone; the Vertu Signature Touch smartphone; a Leica M Edition 60. Tearing open his gifts, he becomes increasingly incensed and starts complaining loudly to his parents. He wanted a silver drone, not a black one; the phone's holder is only in calfskin, which is nowhere near cool enough; and the 35mm f/1.4 ASPH lens on the Leica is all wrong for the kind of photographs he wants to take. Along the corridor, the second twin wakes up to find a large pile of manure steaming away in the corner of his bedroom. Excited, he races off to find his parents. "Oh, thank you, thank you!" he exclaims, excitedly hugging them both. "Where have you hidden the pony?" Ask yourself which twin you would rather hang out with, and which one is more likely to get on successfully in life.

A good repotter needs the determination of an optimist to find the potential upside in any situation, however ostensibly grim, scary, or intimidating. No one is pretending that you can always feel or react like Pollyanna on steroids, especially when your repotting plans go awry, the challenges seem overwhelming, or the nagging fear of failure reasserts its debilitating presence. However, the 3 Rs—Routines, Reframes, and Rituals—are always allies at hand, ready to buoy up your spirits and guide you back on track when things begin to go pear-shaped.

Ensure that you embed all those healthy new routines into your repotted life as swiftly and as firmly as possible. In my case, instead of driving or taking cabs or public transportation in London, I was soon cycling and walking between five and ten miles a day. However daunting the new challenges that I was then obliged to confront, at least I was in far better physical and mental shape to be able to cope with them. Remember making your own list of the positive new routines that you want to implement? Now is a good time to distill all the disparate learnings associated with your new sense of direction into a simplified three-point game plan. The key routines that I found most helpful to embed at this stage included:

1. A Wellness and Well-Being routine, including a commitment to more physical exercise and a well-balanced diet.

2. A Purpose routine, including activities designed to help you achieve the greater personal or professional satisfaction that generated your initial decision to repot.

3. A Community routine, which will probably include not only keeping in touch with people you already know but also engaging with new people and activities that encourage you to challenge and stretch yourself.

Routines do the job only if they are sustainable and consistent with your newly repotted life. To ensure that you adhere to the routine you wish to embed, it's important to add a specific milestone to each category. In terms of Wellness, for instance, commit to doing something as simple as taking the stairs as opposed to the elevator at work, or getting up thirty minutes earlier than absolutely necessary every morning in order to give yourself time to think, exercise, or meditate.

With respect to Purpose, commit to engaging in one activity a day that moves you closer to your personal or professional aspirations—even if it involves something as banal as systematically journaling or filing away your daily learnings in a safe place from which they're easily retrievable.

As for Community, how about committing to something that helps connect you to something bigger than yourself? Volunteering, joining a group, or supporting a cause, if only online, are just a few of the more obvious options.

Our old friend "reframing" is always around to lend support. When things you've planned for aren't working out the way you'd hoped, it's all too easy to start catastrophizing and assuming that everything is going to hell in a handcart. When that happens, I can never help thinking of *Minder*, a TV series popular in the UK throughout the eighties and nineties. Whenever confronted with an almighty cock-up, dodgy businessman Arthur Daley would remain typically unfazed. "Could we be the punters," he instantly reframed on such occasions, "to turn this debacle into an earner?" Learn how to turn things around and, like Arthur, flip the debacle into a straight-up bacle. And, the most powerful technique of all, learn to laugh at yourself.

My arrival in the Land of the Free had been welcomed by a third-degree interrogation, an earthquake, and a borderline hallucinogenic experience. I could reasonably have interpreted these as omens of an inauspicious start. On the contrary, however, I decided to reframe these episodes into positive metaphors for my own repotting narrative: a period of questioning, followed by an upheaval, followed by an alternative take on reality.

Now this might sound rather counterintuitive given that you're trying to move on, but be sure to retain any old rituals that are still meaningful and offer comfort to you. Most cultures and religions have rites of passage or rituals to mark the transitions from one stage of life to the next. In our secular society, we seem to have lost many of them, but rituals function as anchors and keep us feeling secure whenever uncertainty is swirling around us. Traditional, religious rites might work best for you but there's a lot to be said for creating your own go-to rituals. In terms of prayer, for example, I prefer to focus my contemplative efforts on the issue or the person involved rather than invoking celestial intervention. It's not that I'm trying to disintermediarize God, it's just that I find my own technique more helpful. If you've developed any personalized practice, rite, or ritual—whether it involves your runes, your Kara bracelet, or your worry beads—keep at it. Like a child with a comfort blanket, when you're confronting great change, it's reassuring to have the company of a few familiar friends.

GET BACK ON TRACK

Can you remember your first day at school? That terrible churning sensation in the pit of your stomach, the awful feeling that you might be sick all over your new shoes, the desperate yearning to be safely back at home with your mother? That is precisely how I felt when faced with my first day, except that I was sixty-five years old, my mother was over five-and-a-half thousand miles away, and this, for heaven's sake, was Stanford!

I found myself, one cold, bright, blue Northern Californian morning, awash with conflicting sentiments. Twelve months after my potbound epiphany in London, here I was on my first day in Silicon Valley, citadel of the world's most innovative, transformational, and disruptive technologies. Here I was in the springtime of my senility, about to embark on my first day at the USA's most uncompromisingly thrusting and competitive university. Here I was at Stanford. What in God's name was I doing?

I had worked out that Palm Drive, the eponymously fringed road that runs straight from the university's sandstone sentinels to the Stanford Oval, was a brisk fifteen-minute walk toward my destination on campus. Ten minutes into the journey, fidgety with first-day nerves, I decided to double-confirm the directions on my phone and began the usual rummaging in various pockets of my jacket: a London travel pass, a local library card, and an unwrapped Fox's glacier mint of indeterminate vintage now cocooned in a ball of fluff. *Damn!* I had left my phone back at the apartment and, with it, the details of my entire day's schedule. Terrified that I had not memorized exactly where I needed to be and when, I was tempted to race back and retrieve it. But a swift glance at my watch (the Jurassic single-function device still favored by individuals of my era) confirmed that there wasn't time. I was destined to spend my first day at Stanford, *Stanford of all places*, in the gut-wrenching isolation of my own internet-free bubble. I felt sickeningly at sea. Suddenly I was back at university, half a century before, an anxious eighteen-year-old threading her way along unfamiliar windswept streets toward her very first lecture.

Get a grip! The voice of experience began to kick in. A temporarily misplaced phone? What did that matter in the grand scheme of things? I had negotiated the rarefied heights of a ferociously female-unfriendly Cambridge in the early seventies with nothing but an A4 pad, a packet of pens, and a box of Carmen heated hair rollers. Surely I could survive for a few hours, unconnected, without hyperventilating myself to hysteria? Emboldened, I carried on up the drive until I arrived at a set of crossroads. Somewhere over to the left was the Stanford Graduate School of Business, where I was heading. Off to the right lay Stanford's Cantor Arts Center with its adjacent Rodin Sculpture Garden. I glanced at my single-function device again. I still had time for a cultural diversion.

I ended up alone in the garden in the company of a dozen or so Rodin sculptures. Set against the strawberry-blond hues of the nearby museum, the greenish patina of their weathered bronze was warmly welcoming but, despite the interesting agonies depicted by various prostrate figures, I did not stop to contemplate. Instead, I felt my gaze drawn irresistibly toward a canvas of human agony, of the figures writhing in pain in Rodin's monumental sculpture *The Gates of Hell*. From each side of this massive portal, the figures of Adam and Eve surveyed the mayhem that their own mis-behavior had unleashed. Sin, hell, confusion . . . it was all playing out here among the figures struggling to escape from the bronze in which they had been cast forever: the tortured souls of Dante's *Inferno*, Rodin's inspiration.

"Abandon all hope, you who enter here"—so runs the warning across the entrance to Dante's Gates of Hell, but that was not the reference that came to me on my initial day at Stanford. Suddenly I was back in the seventies, on my very first day at college, furiously scribbling notes during the inaugural lecture on Dante's *Divine Comedy*: "Midway in the journey of our life . . ." Here it was again—one of my all-time favorite tales—the journey of Dante, my old, familiar friend, lost and in need of help.

Buried in thought, I suddenly realized the time. Anxious not to be late on my first day, I picked up the pace as I made my way across the Oval toward the Graduate School of Business. The sun was breaking through as shoals of MBA students, bleary-eyed from pilot projects and partying, converged to attend class. Walking toward Community Courtyard, I spotted a Graduate School of Business information plaque. "An Epicenter of Enterprise," it proclaimed, encouraging beer-pong-hungover GSB students to: "Change Lives, Change Organizations, Change the World." But what caught my eye was a smaller italicized paragraph in its bottom left-hand corner. It was a quote from Ernest C. Arbuckle, dean of the school between 1958 and 1968, and he seemed to be speaking directly to me:

Repotting, that's how you get new bloom . . .
you should have a plan of accomplishment
and when that is achieved, you should be
willing to start off again.

The idea of "starting off again" is bound to seem daunt-ing. But while it is perfectly understandable to feel anxious about the changes you're making to your life on your repot-ting journey, there comes a time when you'll feel ready to embrace the excitement of the fresh possibilities now on offer. Moving on from the accomplishments you've worked hard to achieve over a lifetime is never easy. It's inevita-ble that the skills, experiences, and education that you've acquired thus far have become part of your core identity, the label that you use to think about yourself and that you use to identify yourself to others. It is very tempting, there-fore, to keep defaulting to the person you were before you engaged on your repotting journey. But the sooner you can move on from the things that previously defined you, the sooner you'll experience the freedom of exploration and the fun of finding new "bedding-in" fellows.

Reading that inscription, I felt the morning's fears evaporate. This was where I belonged. It was time to dis-pel my remaining anxieties, allow my curiosity full rein, and embrace all the new, exhilarating, and unexpected opportunities for which I'd been clearing space. I had come to be repotted.

TRY NEW THINGS

Moving on is tough because, quite often in life, we don't know what we want, we simply want what we know. If we want to branch out and experience new possibilities, we just have to give those new things a try and be prepared to deal with what happens. Yes, we might make a poor choice, but so what? Scans of some of the world's greatest works of art have uncovered innumerable examples of so-called *pentimenti*. These "acts of repentance" are traces of earlier versions of the painting hidden beneath a layer or even several layers of paint on a canvas and bear witness to the many changes, alterations, and corrections made by the artist during the painstaking process of producing a masterpiece. As we summon up the courage to try new things, it's comforting to think that the initial efforts of even the greatest geniuses are flawed. Repotting involves a series of steps, and *pentimenti* are an important part of making progress throughout that process.

Keep in mind that you shouldn't expect to fall in love with any new activity, role, place, behavior, or way of thinking instantly. I can still recall an evening when my parents came to visit my older brother and me when we were both at university. The restaurant where my brother insisted on going for dinner was his (and, admittedly, also my) favorite Greek restaurant celebrated by impecunious students for its copious portions and cavalier attitude to cholesterol and calories. As manfully we plowed our way through Olympian-size mountains of taramasalata, dolmades, moussaka, kolokythokeftedes, and spanakopita, I stopped to ask my father how he was enjoying his meal. My father, an Irishman of the "don't mess with my carbonized meat and fusion-temperature-boiled vegetables" persuasion, was evasive. Initially I assumed that he was being too polite to complain out of fear of spoiling our evening. Gradually, it occurred to me that my father had never before tasted Greek food and so he didn't actually know whether he liked what he was eating or not. Since the taste of Greek food was so totally unfamiliar to him, that sensation of difference, as opposed to enjoyment, was overwhelming. Only after being forced to eat a few more Greek meals (my brother and I were unyielding in our Spartan determination to expand his culinary tastes) was he able to form any reasonable expectations and to deliver any informed judgment about whether he genuinely liked the food he was eating or not. Tragically, and despite our best efforts, it turned out that he did not, but at least he had a relevant frame of reference with which to evaluate his assessments.

In much the same way, if you don't find a new activity or a new experience instantly compelling, don't be too swift to judge or too easily inclined to give up on it. Give everything you elect to try a fair crack of the whip. Even if it's grueling and involves massive commitment—like working out or studying for a qualification—you'll eventually realize whether or not it's for you by gauging your own levels of satisfaction. If what you're now endeavoring to do is generally making you feel happy, energized, or fulfilled, the chances are that you've hit pay dirt. If not, take heart from my father's Greek-restaurant experience and keep an open mind until you're able to make an informed decision on whether something is right for you.

LEARN TO FAIL FAST

Although repotting involves an openness to trying new things, there's never any point in forcing yourself to do something that affords you no satisfaction, you're not cut out for, or you're simply not enjoying. As discussed earlier, no one wants to fall at the first hurdle, but how can you tell when you're beating a dead horse? It is inevitable that some of the new activities, experiences, and routines you try will prove to be misguided. You may then be tempted to make the debilitating mistake of feeling guilty when you subsequently throw in the towel. If you've given a new venture your best shot and it fails to find resonance with you, don't waste endless amounts of time agonizing about it. Why beat yourself up? That's classic potbound behavior! The world should pay tribute to towel-throwers. Indeed, if ever I attain canonization, and it's unlikely given my track record, I'd like to be venerated as the "Patron Saint of Giving Up" or even "Saint Frances of Failing Fast." Because if you're going to fail—and you sometimes will—it's so much better to fail fast.

With its emphasis on extensive testing and incremental development, the Fail Fast philosophy is tailor-made for repotters at this bedding-in stage. It's a philosophy that helps you assess whether the idea you have has any value at all and whether it's worth pursuing further. It also helps you realize that the knowledge you gain from your failed attempts will actually increase the probability of your eventual success. I've found that the key benefit of failing fast is that it helps you shift your thinking from the requirement of competence to the deeper and far more mature search for meaning. When you're prepared to Fail Fast, the question of "*How* should I do certain things?" morphs into the far more relevant question of "*Why* am I doing these things?" At this point, you're beginning to trade up from the realms of mere knowledge to the far more rarefied heights of wisdom.

Herein, perhaps, lies the resolution to the eternal Fail Fast versus Dig In dilemma. Ask yourself whether you're doing something merely to acquire expertise, experience, or validation for its own sake (and there's nothing wrong in that) or whether you're trying to find meaning in whatever it is you do. If you focus your repotting quest exclusively on increasing your competence, extending your range of experiences, or broadening your network, you'll probably want to try all sorts of different, unrelated things, and you'll likely find that the Fail Fast philosophy works best for you. If you're ready to focus on finding something meaningful more quickly, and since both your time and talent are finite, then you'll probably want to narrow your search to things that check more specific boxes. And once you find the right pot for you, that's when you should persevere and really Dig In.

As part of my research into the benefits of intergenerational learning, and as a particularly helpful exercise in the art of Failing Fast, I was encouraged to take full advantage of the vast gamut of courses on offer at Stanford. Clearly, there were some courses that were off-limits. The School of Medicine, for example, could not reasonably be expected to welcome neophytes desirous of chancing their arm at a bit of DIY open-heart surgery. Apart from a few exclusions, however, I could choose to follow courses in whatever spiked my interest. From aeronautics to astrophysics and from ethics to engineering: I felt like a kid in a candy store as I pored over the available options. Tempted though I was, I was determined not to default too easily into the familiar comfort of the liberal arts. Searching for a suitable synaptic stretch, I signed up for a course on Deep Learning.

It was late afternoon and already the shadows were falling as I arrived at the SAPP Center for Science Teaching and Learning. The modern, tiered auditorium was already packed as I took my seat in the very back row right next to the exit doors. Observing the assembled audience of students, it was difficult not to start feeling distinctly ill at ease. *O brave new world, that has such people in it!* As I watched this parallel universe simultaneously scanning a dozen programs on the split screens of their MacBooks, I tried to calm myself with the verbal assurance the lecturer had given me that this would be a mere 101 walk-in-the-park introductory sort of class. For that reason and, exhausted after a full day on campus, I had left my own laptop and heavy backpack in a locker at the Law School. Now, I found myself in an auditorium crammed with some of the smartest scientists of a generation—armed with nothing more than my dog-eared notebook and badly bleeding pen.

Just moments before the start of the lecture, a rather disheveled young man arrived, and I shuffled sideways a few seats across the back row to cede him my prime position next to the exit. As the lecture proceeded, my head began to throb as we dug ever deeper into artificial neural networks. It might have been at "posterior probability," or perhaps at "stochastic gradient descent," or quite possibly at "particle swarm optimization," but at some point around thirty minutes in, my brain stopped communicating with my pen. The sea of students before me began to undulate in time with the thumping rhythm now pounding away in my skull. On the beat, I snapped my notebook shut and, with what I hoped might pass for an inscrutable expression, slid silently across the back row toward the exit.

Observing my crablike maneuver, the young man who had taken my seat obligingly picked up his stuff and stood. With a cavalier flourish, he opened the door to let me pass before unexpectedly following me out of the auditorium. The door swung shut and, for a moment, he stopped and stared at me, obviously sizing up this strange outlier of a superannuated student. Shamefacedly shoveling my belongings back into my bag, I was intrigued to see the young man's face light up on completion of his computations. "Too bloody basic, eh?" he said, flashing me a conspiratorial smile. Nonplussed, I nodded. Then he nodded. We both nodded. "Yeah, too bloody basic for me too!" he said, contentedly confirming his analysis. And with that, he gave me a triumphantly superior high five and wandered off into the evening.

I was unsure whether to laugh or applaud—quite possibly I should have done both. I'd been expecting him to assume (correctly) that I was totally out of my depth in attacking such a hardcore subject. Clearly, however, I'd underestimated this undergraduate who'd now succeeded in putting my own preconceptions to shame. Given my advanced age, I'd been convinced that this sharp young computer scientist would instantly write me off as a dabbling time-waster. On the contrary, he had made no such deprecating judgments. He'd elected instead to give me the benefit of the doubt: Either I must be some expert covertly checking the quality of the teaching or, like him, a fellow student ahead of the class. Absolved by his elegant, if erroneous, summation, I felt liberated from any guilt I might have felt in deciding to call it a day. I was glad to have given this Brave New World a swift visit but now felt free to move on in search of different climes more suited to my own proclivities. Far more important than any other consideration, this was a key lesson in intergenerational learning. On the whole, I realized, young people are far less ready to judge. More older folk should be ready to return the compliment.

BE OPEN TO NEW PEOPLE AND PERSPECTIVES

To be a truly successful repotter, you have to be prepared to expose yourself to all sorts of new people and ideas, to be ready to laugh at yourself on occasion, and to understand that your way of looking at things may no longer be valid and that, however accomplished you are, you can always learn from other people. Humility, humanity, and a sense of humor are crucial ingredients in the repotting mix, along with tolerance and emotional intelligence. Being tolerant most certainly does not mean your passive acceptance of alternative viewpoints, but it does mean remaining open to new experiences, responding to disagreement with equanimity, and demonstrating patience in trying to understand all sides of other people's often complex and multifaceted situations.

If you think that all this sounds like a tall order, you're right. No one ever said that repotting was easy but, as already noted, the more you practice, the better you get. As a child, you were probably taught that before passing judgment on anyone else, you should try to see the world as the other person sees it by first walking a mile in their shoes. As the old joke goes, the worst that can happen is that you end up a mile away with the bonus of a free pair of shoes. It may be empathy fatigue but, on bad days, you may end up feeling that you've walked so many miles in other people's shoes that you've ended up losing your own. Why is it, you wonder, that no one else is reciprocating the nonjudgmental favor by walking around in yours? Lighten up! This is a classic example of poor-me potbound self-absorption, and you must do your best to resist it. As a determined repotter, you'll not only learn to get along with most other people in spite of their differences, failings, and idiosyncrasies, but you might even find yourself reveling in the experience, and certainly you'll grow from it. Of course, you'd have to be a saint not to be irritated by other folk on occasion, but learn to keep your outrage powder dry to wage the truly worthwhile wars.

As the weeks went by at Stanford, I felt the liberation of judgment after judgment, preconception after preconception, certainty after certainty falling by the wayside. The accumulated strata of a lifetime of received wisdoms and all-too-often-unchallenged notions began to melt away under the sanitizing pressure of self-scrutiny. It was if all the dead wood of my previous life had been stripped away and I was being forced to rebuild myself from scratch. Perhaps the USA was proving such fertile soil because Americans themselves are natural repotters. Americans often seem to act as if everything has to be done and dusted within one generation. To other nationalities, Americans always appear to be in a hurry to get things done, to move on once those projects have been accomplished, and to have a crack at something else. While researching his treatise *Democracy in America*, the French historian Alexis de Tocqueville observed, "The American has no time to tie himself to anything." And that, I believe, is the great difference between USA and Europe: The Americans have always been in transition. For me, a British woman in deep middle age, it was revivifying to osmose the American enthusiasm to identify, try, and test new approaches, a mindset universally in evidence at Stanford. Sadly, it's just not possible to escape to the Californian sunshine every time you need a reset, but you can replicate similar degrees of enthusiasm whenever you challenge yourself to try something different, commit to learn from the experience, and not fret too much about the outcome.

Whenever you seriously question your preconceived ideas and start to explore new perspectives, it's only natural to revisit those key periods of your life when you formulated your current thinking. My arrival at a new university inevitably took me back to my original higher-education experience, which could not have been more different. For starters, when I went to Cambridge way back in 1970, there were ten men to every one woman. Looked at in a certain light, the odds were very good, although, looked at in another, some of the goods were very odd. Many young men whose exposure to women has been limited to a nanny, a boys' elementary school, and an all-male high school were content to continue in their exclusively men-only sports and drinking clubs. Numerically restricted as we were, we women were distributed among three female-only colleges, and although academic departments, lectures, and supervisions (tutorials) were mixed, accommodation remained rigidly segregated and rules on male guests and visiting hours rigidly applied, if not always quite so rigidly respected.

My first encounter with an all-gender restroom at Stanford was therefore a liberating sign of the times. Further demonstrations of diversity training emerged as academics half my age asked solicitously how I'd like to be addressed. At first I assumed that they must be concerned that the casual use of my first name would seem a trifle infra dig, but it was actually a question of gender fluidity. At the start of any new class, I was intrigued to witness how every individual was encouraged to explain at length and with absolute precision quite how he/she/they wanted to be addressed, understood, and categorized.

It was bewildering for me at first, but as I grew to appreciate more fully the vulnerability and, in some cases, the confusion of so many of the students, I felt ashamed of my initial dismissiveness. As we get older and more set in our ways, it can be hard to abandon our world perspective and all too easy to make light of concerns that we ourselves have always been forced to ignore, suppress, or conceal. It's not only monstrously unfair but also intellectually impoverishing to keep shoehorning different people into the easily disposable boxes of your own preconceived ideas. My diaries covering that initial period are full of facetious entries about selfish snowflake students showily clinging onto their emotional support dogs. As time went by, however, I discovered that these selfsame snowflakes were infinitely more forgiving of a clueless old coot incapable of finding her way around shared Google docs and invariably lost in Excel spreadsheets.

How and when did the intellectual idleness kick in that had resulted in such knee-jerk reactions? At what point did my own capacity for critical analysis give way to lazy caricature and generalization? You've got to catch yourself on the slippery slope of sloppy thinking before you end up in the ever-swelling ranks of filter-bubble bigots. I realized that I had to give my smug sexagenarian self a good talking-to. Increasingly, I took time to listen to, work with, and learn from an ever-widening range of different people. I waited until I had enough information before forming any kind of view about them and, even then, was constantly reviewing my initial assessments. If you ever catch yourself falling into the pernicious instant-opinion trap, just stop and give yourself a good mental kick. Then take time to do your due diligence before you react. Not only will you make interesting and unexpected new friends, but you'll also save yourself a lot of U-turns on the road to repotting.

SUIT UP AND PLAY AGAIN

Over the course of my first week in Palo Alto, I came to realize that there were quite a few other Distinguished Careers Institute fellows holed up in the same apartment block as I was. Every one of them looked poised and calm, as if—unlike me—they had segued seamlessly into this new start-from-the-bottom-again phase of life. Gradually, however, as I got to know them better, I realized that we were all very much in the same boat. I don't know whether it was serendipity or the process by which we were selected— probably a combination of both—but somehow this group of diverse individuals from all over the world and drawn from a wide range of sectors shared the same repotting impulse. We each had our own individual reasons for deciding to uproot, and we were all unsure of exactly where we would end up, but we were on the same path and—better still—we had the enormous good fortune of traveling along it together.

One of the most enduringly transformative exercises that I undertook at Stanford was the requirement to share my "Life Story" in a twenty-minute presentation. When I tell you that each member of our fellowship cohort, which was packed with many highly successful and competitive individuals, was required to share their personal history, it sounds like a gilt-edge guaranteed recipe for some truly ghastly one-upmanship. Counterintuitive though it might sound, this exercise did more than anything else to bind us all together with a sense of mutual empathy and community. Digging deep, often with painful honesty, to establish what it was about ourselves that had remained the same throughout our lives and what it was that had happened to us that had precipitated change, proved to be a profoundly cathartic experience. No matter what our background and no matter who we were, we all recognized each other as fellow pilgrims traveling together on a quest for personal transformation.

A few common threads emerged clearly from the glorious cornucopia of personal stories that we shared—the highs and lows of life from an extraordinary range of experiences, from a beauty and cosmetics pioneer to a bank founder, from an orchestral conductor to a state attorney, and from a biotech entrepreneur to a ballerina. Listening to the brutally and endearingly honest admissions of setbacks, heartbreaks, and disasters liberally scattered across lives that ultimately met with success, it struck me that many people may be blessed with natural talent, but the gift of natural talent will propel you only so far. If their stories were anything to go by, the most crucial lesson that every member of my repotting family had assimilated was that hard work, discipline, and conscientiousness are better guarantors of personal and professional success than any amount of raw talent. And all these individuals were determined to leverage these selfsame attributes to repot for the next stage of their lives. Irrespective of your area of endeavor and whatever your life story, the same holds true for you. No one will ever win a gold medal for being organized, responsible, and practical, but these remain the key blue-ribbon repotting credentials that will drive you to keep commitments, follow through, and achieve success in your chosen field.

Whatever point you've reached in your own repotting journey, I believe that the Life Story is a valuable exercise to try for yourself. Start by writing down a concise version of your own life story, with an emphasis on continuity, causality, and change. A few prompts might include questions along the following lines: What is it about you that has stayed the same? What is it about you that has changed and why? Are there any recurrent threads or guiding lights that run through your life story? Think of it as a narrative that makes sense of who you are and what you've done in the past, and that encourages you to consider what you are capable of achieving in the future. Although life is lived forward, it is understood backward and, with the benefit of hindsight, it's surprisingly easy to create a coherent narrative around your life thus far. With the addition of a dash of repotting optimism, I suspect that you'll also be able to construct meaning and a positive perspective around your life journey to date. Remember that meaning is not something that you stumble across by chance. It's something that you must build for yourself out of your past, your experiences, your talents, the values you hold dear, the people you love, and the things you believe in. You are the only one who has the right to construct your unique narrative—so make sure that your own life story has meaning for you. This understanding, in addition to the energy unleashed by memories of problems solved, obstacles overcome, and general ability to survive will, in turn, reinforce your determination to create further meaning and purpose in your repotted future.

As I listened to my new friends presenting their own narratives, I was struck by the fact that no matter how distinguished they had been in their previous lives and careers, they were all now determined to turn their former personal and professional success into some deeper form of significance. At a time in life when many people decide to put their feet up, this was a fellowship of folk who bore witness to the view of former US president Bill Clinton that "America has never been a retirement party. It's a constant effort to suit up and play again." It certainly *was* a constant effort, however, especially at the beginning, and my sexagenarian synapses often struggled to stay the course of a daily schedule that would have floored me in my twenties. In order to stay on top of their onerous workloads, younger students I knew would often pull all-nighters. Frequently I found myself hard-pressed to pull all-dayers. In the initial stages of my deep developmental disruption, I could regularly be caught taking afternoon naps in the Bender Room of Cecil H. Green Library and, without fear of scandal, can openly admit to sleeping with at least two Nobel Prize winners during that period. In other words, find time for self-compassion, especially when you're negotiating times of serious upheaval and change. It needn't be an expensive treatment: Often a nap on the couch will do.

PRACTICE SOME FORM OF MINDFULNESS

With all the associated stresses and anxieties, negotiating change can be exhausting. If possible, you'd do well to consider your own wellness and well-being more assiduously when bedding into the next phase of your life. Like a healthy diet, the concept of mindfulness is simple to understand but devilishly difficult to practice. The trick is learning how to anchor yourself in the present, recognize what's happening in your mind right now (identify feelings of fear, anger, jealousy, sadness, etc.), and respond to that emotion consciously rather than subconsciously. Focusing on the present can be hard, especially given our natural tendency either to dwell on the past or to plan for the future, in addition to our monkey mind's natural predisposition to race off in pursuit of distraction.

It is not the purpose of this book to give you a full course in mindfulness, but let me share the relatively straightforward concept of "noting," to which I was introduced by my wonderful mindfulness teacher. Noting involves applying a soft mental label to your sensations and feelings. For example, imagine that you're itching. Instead of immediately and instinctively scratching the itch, you simply note the fact that you're itching and say to yourself, "I'm itching." The point of this exercise is to short-circuit the mindless chain reaction in which you habitually jump from stimulus to reaction without pause for any conscious thought. Apply the same process to feelings such as fear or anger, and you can in time learn to stop for a moment, note how you are feeling, and modulate your emotional response accordingly. With this simple technique, you can dial down the emotional heat, and this will work wonders for your overall well-being.

I used to dismiss mindfulness as a complete waste of time—up there in the Pointless League alongside housework, attempting to understand the offside rule, and arguing with adolescents. Perhaps excessive exposure to various apps purveying McMindfulness, those forms of Mindfulness Lite eviscerated of the core belief system that ought to underpin the practice, led me to think that mindfulness was little more than a cynical commodification of the blindingly obvious. However, feeling overwhelmed by the demands of my freshly repotted life and attempting to follow my rule of trying new things, I decided to do what any self-respecting Californian stressee would do and signed up for a course of mindfulness-based stress reduction.

Compared to all the frankly lunatic fads that I tried in Silicon Valley, including yoga with goats and "equin-inity" (mindfulness with horses . . . believe me, I'm not making this up), basic mindfulness had begun to sound an eminently sensible option. It also chimed in well with the process of repotting, given its regular practitioners' belief in its power to control anxieties, ward against negative behaviors, and enhance concentration and focus. Ready by now to give most things the benefit of the doubt, I found a highly recommended teacher and duly presented myself at class.

What a revelation! As I was increasingly discovering, the more you talk to other people and hear about the problems they are trying to manage, the faster the stress of your own paltry melodrama fades to complete insignificance. More interesting still, it seemed that an entire cadre of hardheaded scientific and engineering folk—the sort of people I'd once have thought would dismiss the value of such pursuits—were fervent practitioners and championed the benefits publicly. I was intrigued to hear one world-class engineer explaining how mindfulness had helped him focus more effectively on his military technology work for the US government. To me, it all seemed so confusingly Silicon Valley. "Hurrah for the wonders of mindfulness-based stress reduction! Now let's go and nuke North Korea!"

PLUG YOURSELF INTO YOUR COMMUNITY

At every stage of life, as you move from the disruption and pain of uprooting, through the discipline and process of repotting, and onward in the direction of purposeful new growth, you need community support. At certain critical inflection points, such as parenthood, illness, unemployment, or bereavement, you may need more help than at other periods, and your social engagement and networks will change over time to reflect changing personal and professional needs. What never changes, however, is the fundamental need for other people because we humans are inherently social beings. From an evolutionary perspective, our very survival depends on strong attachments to our caregivers, and we're born preprogrammed to bond to others.

On a personal level, you start off life as a member of a family, and with that, you automatically plug into the wider nexus of your ethnic, national, religious, and cultural tribes. You then move on to join communities of friends and acquaintances associated with stages and areas of your life, including school, college, local neighborhood, interests, hobbies, teams, and political persuasions. Professionally, you probably join a team or an organization. In addition, you may decide to become a member of communities that represent your interests, protect your rights, advocate on behalf of your profession or industry or, in the case of awarding bodies, ensure the highest standards in your qualifications and continuous professional development.

Throughout your personal and professional life, your social engagement and connectedness continue to have profound implications for your overall well-being. They help provide you with a sense of security, self-esteem, physical, mental, and cognitive health, as well as a general satisfaction with life. As I know from my own DCI experience, repotters in particular benefit from the support, protection, nurture, and safe environment offered by their community, especially during periods when they're experimenting with new ideas on how best to live and work.

A few months into my fellowship, my ninety-seven-year-old mother passed away back in England. She had fallen ill with pneumonia just as I was leaving the UK, which had made my departure infinitely more painful. Her story was that of an entire generation of men and women whose lives were hallmarked by uncomplaining fortitude and sense of duty. At the age of nineteen, she had volunteered to join the Women's Auxiliary Air Force, served throughout World War II, and, having trained as a teacher after the war, went on to marry my father. She spent the rest of her life managing a doctor's practice and patients, looking after a brood of four demanding children, and supporting me, my brothers, and our own children through the ups and downs of our endless sagas until the day she died.

Like many who had suffered the privations of her generation, my mother had no time for whining. During the interminably long summer vacations of my childhood, when television was still a novelty and internet access well beyond even the fevered imagination of science fiction, the gray drizzle of the northwest of England would occasionally get me down, and I would unwisely complain of boredom and a desperate desire to be anywhere else. My mother only ever made three suggestions: "Read a book!" "Tidy your drawers!" or, in extreme cases of adolescent temper, "Count your blessings!" At the beginning of every year, I still write that final exhortation on the front page of my desk diary. Not only does it make me smile at the thought of my mother, but as anyone who has lived through a war knows only too well, it reminds me that everything, including family, friends, health, and wealth, can be snatched away overnight. I also think it has an important role to play in the repotting mindset. Research has shown that being grateful for what you have can actively alter your brain chemistry and generate a cheerful outlook. It might feel fake to begin with, but—believe the neuroscientists on this one—it ends up being real.

My mother missed her opportunity to go to college; she never sat on a board, sought public office, or created a multimillion-dollar business. But as I grew up, I could see the huge impact that her concept of service, her selflessness, and her inalienable good humor had on everyone around her. I think she knew naturally what medical, psychological, and sociological researchers supported by Stanford's Center on Longevity and Distinguished Careers Institute now tell us— that the three things in life that matter most are wellness, purpose, and community.

No one can ever prepare you for the desolation of waking up to find yourself an orphan. However old you are, you feel untethered from your moorings. I was blessed to be swept up in the empathetic embrace of my genuinely supportive DCI community. The kindness went way beyond cards and words of condolence as my new friends opened their hearts to me with all the healing power of a caring, extended family. I realized that almost unconsciously I had succeeded in building myself a new type of "repotting network"—a peer group suited not only to who I was but also to who I wanted to be. And at this moment of loss, I realized that I had also gained a genuinely supportive community of new friends.

The need for social connection does not fade as you grow older, even though the ways in which you view and use your social networks and your levels of social connectedness tend to change as you move through different phases of your life. Spearheaded by the inspirational Professor Laura Carstensen, extensive research by Stanford's Center on Longevity has discovered that feeling socially isolated presents as great a risk for premature death as smoking a half a packet of cigarettes a day. Equally concerning, research has also shown that as many as sixty million Americans feel sufficiently isolated for them to identify loneliness as a major source of unhappiness in their lives. Even more surprising, it also appears that, above poverty level, the availability of money doesn't contribute significantly to happiness. Instead, community and all that community implies in terms of companionship, family, friendship, and social support remains the precious, intangible asset that you most require for your overall well-being.

While I had managed to build myself a repotting community without ever really thinking about it, I have since come across some good advice for taking a more strategic approach to the process. Flicking through an American sports magazine, I chanced on a piece about the Ultimate Fighting Championship legend and mixed martial artist Frank Shamrock. Frank observed that successful fighters all espoused the discipline of "Plus—Minus—Equals." They search out someone better (+) from whom they can learn, someone lesser (–) whom they can teach, and someone equal (=) against whom they can challenge themselves. That strikes me as a winning formula to adopt—encouraging you to seek out those who can help you achieve your goals, while also prompting you to make an active contribution to the success of others. It also reflects the way that my time at Stanford opened my eyes to the other side of the community coin—not the role that community plays in my life, but the role that I can play in my community. And this in turn led me to revise my understanding of what repotting really means . . .

SUMMARY

1. Be ready to experience doubt and fear. Reframe and embrace your optimism.

2. Learn the power of Failing Fast, but don't expect to know instantly whether something is right or wrong for you.

3. Be curious and tolerant in your dealings with others. Develop your emotional intelligence and do as you would be done by.

4. Create coherence, energy, and optimism by harnessing the power of your own Life Story.

5. Be thankful for talent, but remember that commitment is even more essential.

6. Look after your physical, intellectual, emotional, and spiritual self. Plan to spend time alone and practice some form of quiet contemplation or mindfulness.

7. Seek the support and fellowship of good company. A supportive community makes all the difference. Connection with others is key.

CONCLUSION:
NEW BLOOM

After my transformational time in the USA, I returned to the same house, the same neighborhood, and the same friends that I had previously bade farewell to in London. It was tough to leave the luminescent light of California to face the gritty grayness of an English winter, and the thought of the newfound extended family that I had left behind filled me with a terrible sadness. There had been sleepless nights and tearful goodbyes, but deep inside I had known that it was time to go home. On the surface, it might have seemed that very little in my life had changed. I hadn't taken Silicon Valley by storm, created a billion-dollar start-up, discovered a cure for cancer, or won a Nobel Prize. But I was no longer feeling potbound—and the insights I'd acquired on my repotting journey had helped me formulate a completely different take on life and a totally different mindset.

Returning home to England, now feeling rewired rather than retired, I'd anticipated that it would take some time to readjust and process everything that I'd learned and lived through at Stanford. As with all repotted plants, however, I'd also accepted that you need to have a little patience before new growth emerges, leaves unfurl, and a glorious new bloom finally bursts into blossom.

It was therefore hardly ideal to leave the Land of the Free only to find myself almost immediately immured in the lockdown of COVID London. I hadn't spent the last few years in Silicon Valley, however, without osmosing the benefits of a swift mental reframe. What better use of any period of enforced isolation than an opportunity to reflect? What conclusions could be drawn from my participation in the extraordinary sociological experiment from which I'd just emerged?

I had, of course, a welter of notes and files from the work I'd done around the issue of longevity and was more or less up to speed on most of the latest thinking on wellness and well-being. All these were tangible outcomes, however, as my laptop's exploding hard drive could readily attest. The far more valuable benefits that I could feel and that were now sustaining me were of a far more ineffable nature. How can you quantify intangibles such as flexibility, resilience, and curiosity? Or the joy of problem-solving? How can you put a value on self-reliance, humor, or empathy? How do you measure the benefits derived from both meaningful connections and the ability to sit happily alone? At a time in life when most people are experiencing the gradual impoverishment of loss—be it the loss of physical strength and faculties, the loss of family and friends, or the loss of the organizing principle and status associated with the conventional world of work—I was feeling enriched by the resources that my recent repotting experience had obliged me to assimilate.

At this stage, you might also want to take stock of the progress you've made so far and the fresh insights you've acquired. Cast your mind back to those gloomy potbound days and compare the emotions that assailed you then with your current physical, mental, and emotional state. If your repotting plan involved improving your physical wellness and well-being, for instance, have you succeeded in reaching your targets? If so, can you leverage this sense of achievement to ensure that you keep up the good work? If not, try calling up the intense feelings of dissatisfaction and discomfort that made you want to make improvements in the first place and use these to motivate yourself to get back on track again. Did you promise yourself to acquire a new skill? If so, are you satisfied with what you've achieved thus far and can you use your enhanced expertise as a confidence-building measure to inspire you to go even further? And if your repotting plan involved extracting yourself from a negative relationship, situation, or habit, consider whether you've truly managed to break free or if there's still some residual tidying up, pruning, and deadheading to be done. Make a note of the intangible as well as the tangible benefits you have reaped thus far. You might not have reached the goals you originally set out for yourself, but you'll certainly have opened up your mind to new possibilities and expanded your horizons in the process. You'll have also progressed to being what every purposeful repotter aspires to be: a work in perpetual and purposeful progress.

After my time at Stanford, working with some of the brightest young people on the planet, I felt energized to continue undertaking new ventures, no longer embarrassed by the prospect of messing things up or of making a fool of myself. Denied the possibility of "in-person" engagement during extended periods of lockdown, I decided to do the next best thing and enthusiastically signed up for a wide range of online courses—from bridge to boxing, calligraphy to coding, and philosophy to film studies. Whereas, along with half the locked-up nation, I might easily have defaulted to the demon drink or baking sourdough bread, I found support in a far more nurturing pursuit—my renewed enthusiasm for lifelong learning. More fulfilling still, inspired by how powerfully supportive my DCI tribe had proved to be,

I plugged into my local community, determined to see how I could contribute, if only by helping out with groceries or supplying laptops to disadvantaged children struggling with the challenges of homeschooling. The benefits of reaching out cut both ways: I am now something of an expert on damson jam, data security, and default factory settings.

Repotting, I was beginning to realize, is a never-ending endeavor. I would never be done with my changes until I was repotted six feet deep. Many of us will have experienced how game-changing and revivifying repotting benefits can be, but we all need to continue nurturing our new growth and ensure there's room for further development or we'll end up becoming potbound again. And if you do, it's not the end of the world. Just uproot and start over again.

REFRAMING REPOTTING

However beneficial personal development may be, most repotters will end up understanding that their personal growth is an asset even further enhanced when exercised in, or in the service of, a wider community. In other words, repotting is not just a matter for individuals; it should be built into the fabric of society.

As for many people during the worldwide lockdown, my months of self-isolation were regularly punctuated by Zoom calls with increasingly distressed friends in increasingly dubious athleisurewear. Everywhere you looked, it seemed that the pandemic was serving to highlight a host of hitherto hidden fissures in a broad range of pots. Across the globe, a host of time-honored practices, beliefs, and behaviors were being challenged and, in many cases, found not to be quite as important or immutable as we'd thought. At such a time of upheaval, I felt fortunate to live within walking distance of Holland Park, one of London's most beautiful public spaces, the northern half of which is covered in semi-wild woodland. Quite why it took a global pandemic for me to appreciate the wondrous resource situated on my own doorstep is for another time, but as country after country reverted to disturbingly isolationist and nationalistic behavior and as the world's supermarkets were plundered of their treasure troves of toilet tissue, the tranquility of the woodland proved profoundly restorative at a time of generalized anxiety.

As the months went by, I began to notice how well the wise old inhabitants of this magic garden were faring compared with the frantic folk muddling along amid the mayhem outside. Neither dependent nor independent, but interdependent, these trees—young, old, and positively ancient—seemed to demonstrate a degree of intergenerational cooperation of which our disrupted world order seemed quite incapable. I became increasingly intrigued by this cooperative ecosystem and wondered how its members might communicate and work together. My research confirmed what I had already begun to intuit: that my new friends, the trees, had important lessons not only for individual repotters, but also for the ways in which repotting might be usefully embraced by society as a whole.

Just like human beings, trees need their own space in order to thrive as individuals. Around the crown of every tree, for instance, there's a slim contour of empty space known as "crown shyness," which is the tree's rather elegant way of telling its fellow forest dwellers to back off. If you take time to observe individual trees in a wood or forest, you'll find that they seem instinctively to respect each other's space and leave gaps between the end of one tree's outermost leaves and the start of another's. In this parallel sylvan universe, however, the overall community is also hard at work and busily pulling together. Dig down, and under the forest floor you'll find another world of infinite biological pathways that connect trees, enable them to exchange information, and allow the forest to function as if it is a single organism. Within the community, "mother" or "hub" trees recognize and communicate with their kin. They support their seedling "children" by providing them with nutrients and by generally shaping future generations. Even more fascinating, it seems that older trees that have suffered disease and injury give the forest community the benefit of this experience by passing on their legacy through gene regulation and defense chemistry.

In addition to all this communal effort, and thanks to a complex web of fungi, different tree species are able to lend food to each other as deficits occur. This makes for a particularly beneficial arrangement between coniferous and deciduous trees, which experience energy deficits during different seasons. With a laudable sense of altruism, fallen trees will often turn themselves into "nurse logs" and continue to contribute to the community by providing "ecological facilitation." As they decay, they offer seedlings shade, nutrients, water, and protection from disease and pathogens, thus providing nurture for the new generation.

What an inspirational template my local park had unveiled for a cohesive and purposeful repotted society! In the wake of my own individual repotting journey—and as a result of my longevity studies—I have come increasingly to wonder why human society seems incapable of harnessing the power of this kind of intergenerational cooperation. Given general increases in life expectancy, I'm convinced that this failure is leading to an ever greater waste of precious, untapped resources. In many first-world countries, once people reach a certain age, they effectively become segregated from the rest of society—detached from the world of employment, no longer living under the same roof as other generations of their family, and expected at best to enjoy a life of leisure or at worst a period of waiting for death, fraught with concerns over dwindling resources, plummeting annuities, and the prospect of penurious old age. Repotting may be able to inject fortunate individuals with a renewed sense of purpose, but just imagine the benefits to modern society as a whole if it could embrace the concept of repotting to help integrate different generations.

How about learning from the tree community to create communication between different age groups that often seem so disconnected from each other? By way of example, research into happiness and purpose in later life shows that older people who mentor and support younger people are three times more likely to be happy than those who don't. Furthermore, it turns out that the two loneliest groups in society are younger people and older people, so it's a win–win solution if such mentorship can foster genuine relationships between the different generations, especially when the mentoring ends up going both ways. And thinking about those heroic "nurse logs"—what a fillip to intergenerational solidarity when the repotting perennials in society recognize that the best contribution they can make to their community is not by constantly trying to assume central roles themselves but by investing in younger people and thereby ensuring that their influence and guidance continue through the lives and work of the next generation. How infinitely more rewarding to live a legacy rather than simply to leave one!

In pockets across the world, transformed and transformational repotters are searching for innovative ways to bring age diversity into schools, colleges, workplaces, communities, and social movements. They are committed to bringing generations together to create intergenerational solutions to serious global problems, from illiteracy to loneliness and from sustainability to social justice. A range of encore careers is emerging that's specifically geared to mixing people of different ages in initiatives of intergenerational and mutually beneficial learning.

Cast around and you'll find inspirational stories and role models such as the retired British judge who became a powerful protagonist in a youth literacy program. His years in court had led him to realize that most of the young offenders he was sentencing had first become involved in crime after being excluded from school for disruptive behavior. On discovering that was often due to illiteracy or undiagnosed dyslexia, he became determined to address the problem. A well-known British journalist left her high-profile job at the *Financial Times* to retrain as a high school teacher and cofounded an educational charity. My own brother, a retired eye surgeon, now devotes much of his time to coaching young doctors in the people skills required to conduct difficult conversations with distressed patients and their families.

Even in the hard-nosed, supercompetitive world of business start-ups, research from the Massachusetts Institute of Technology's *Sloan Management Review* has found that young founders, who often have deep but narrow technical skills and fresh eyes for disruption, can be usefully paired with seasoned leaders. Obviously, no lean, thrusting start-up wants to be saddled with some stuck-in-the-Dark-Ages corporate codger incapable of switching on his own computer and demanding an assistant to fetch his coffee and regular printouts of his emails. Wiser repotting elders, however, are likely to have acquired the leadership skills of interpersonal collaboration and ability to focus on the bigger picture that will make them invaluable to any fledgling business.

Since management style varies more with age than any other characteristic (including organizational position or gender), diversity is maximized by creating an intergenerational workforce and leadership team. Older managers put greater emphasis on core competencies, customer relationships, and other strategic factors central to a company's identity, while younger managers are more focused on the company's positioning in its competitive marketplace and their own positioning for career advancement. This backs up what neuroscientists have suggested for decades: that the younger brain is quicker and more focused, while the older brain is more methodical and holistic. A team full of solely younger people will come to conclusions more quickly but make more mistakes. An older team does just the opposite. A blended team of mixed ages will achieve the best of both worlds.

In other words, enlightened repotters will realize that benefits of any repotting exercise should not merely begin and end with you. Sharing accumulated wisdom, reapplying well-honed skills, and leveraging relevant lived experience will help support families, encourage vibrant, responsive, and responsible business, and lead ideally to a more cohesive and compassionate society.

Thinking back to the day I saw that poor potbound plant on television, I now see that my own views on repotting have changed quite dramatically. At that time, and from the perspective of my deep middle age, I had imagined that the repotting journey I knew I must then undertake would be my last. I had thought, too, that it was an entirely individual process arising out of personal experience and a need for radical change to enable a fuller, richer life. I now realize, of course, that I was seriously mistaken. The process of repotting, if often difficult and occasionally dramatic in its steps, turns out to be continual and never-ending. It also has implications for our relationships not only with ourselves and those closest to us but to the wider community around us and the world at large.

My repotting journey involved shedding much of the "stuff" cluttering my life and moving half a world away, challenging myself physically, intellectually, and spiritually into a fresh way of perceiving the world and thinking about my place in it. Your repotting might be even more radical, although you might decide to stay in the same place and make what might seem to others relatively small changes— to you they could be dramatic and far-reaching. Managing beginnings and endings, seeing familiar things as if for the first time, reassessing old beliefs and notions . . . if there is one gift I could wish for you, like the Grimms' benign fairy godmother, it would be just that—a quiet revolution that embraces change yet safeguards the deservedly constant and unchanging. Above the soil, the plant is still the same genus, but its leaves are glossier and its blooms more startlingly beautiful, all because beneath the surface its roots and tendrils are luxuriating afresh in a nourishing, new environment. And if those tendrils should reach the limits of the new pot and start to turn in on themselves, well, now you know what to do.

Even more than a process or a journey, repotting is a frame of mind, a way of life and a commitment to keep on growing. It's the determination to discover delight in the rich diversity of life, the curiosity to dance with change and the ability to find the fun of good fellowship. It's the treasure trove of gifts that I hope my goddaughter will draw on as she negotiates her expected hundred-year span. I hope that she, and you, will find this book helpful. I also hope that my own experience gives you the impetus you may need to make your own start and even raises the odd wry smile of quite possibly rueful recognition.

Happy repotting!

ACKNOWLEDGMENTS

First and foremost, I would like to thank my fellow repotters at the Distinguished Careers Institute, Stanford. Some of you have become close friends whose lives will be forever intertwined with mine. You know who you are and, however hard you try, there's no getting away from that now! Others have created a lasting impression by encouraging me to question just about everything I thought I knew or ever took for granted. Each and every one of you has inspired me by your commitment to the three pillars of wellness, purpose, and community that inform our common understanding of how best to manage the societal challenge of extended life expectancy in an increasingly volatile world. For the gift of this extraordinary extended family and the enduring benefits I have derived from its collective wisdom, expertise, and kindness, I should like to thank the Institute's visionary founder, Professor Phil Pizzo, former dean of Stanford

University School of Medicine whose empathy, compassion, and insight are now trained on the future of higher education for individuals in later life. My thanks go also to the DCI administrative team, whose indefatigable support was crucial to my successful "bedding down" in the USA. In the area of academic advice and mentoring, I am forever indebted to Professor Laura Carstensen, my faculty adviser and founding director of Stanford's Center on Longevity, for her scholarship, friendship, and inalienable good humor. And to John Evans, Draper Lecturer at Stanford's English Department, my eternal gratitude for breaking a logjam and motivating me to return to writing.

My own understanding of the physical and often underreported mental and emotional trauma involved in uprooting has been reinforced by my dealings with the mobility industry, in particular the European Relocation Association (EuRA). My thanks to Dom Tidey, Tad Zurlinden, and my many friends in the profession who help ease the stress of repotters in the process of relocating around the globe.

In the UK, I would like to thank my friend and much-loved media icon Angela Rippon for her unstinting enthusiasm and encouragement and also for introducing me to key figures in Newcastle's National Innovation Centre for Ageing. My publishers, Elliott & Thompson, have been truly supportive from the moment I discussed my initial ideas for this book with the inimitably generous Lorne Forsyth. Editors Sarah Rigby and Pippa Crane have both very sensibly restrained my wilder excesses and put their hearts and souls into ensuring that this book is of maximum direct and immediate help to the reader. Jill Burrows has done a terrific job of copyediting, never an easy task when the author is fond of making up words of her own. Andrew Sauerwine (Commercial Publishing Company), Luthfa Begum, and Ella Chapman have been huge fun to work with and I am in awe of their genius in terms of branding, marketing, and promulgating the various concepts explored in "repotting." Emma Finnigan has worked her magic as a publicist managing public relations for this book and ensuring the widest possible coverage of the issues involved. In terms of disseminating the overall repotting message, I would also like to pay tribute to my niece, Enya Moriarty, for her help in introducing me to the parallel universe of social media.

Finally, I would like to thank my daughter, Alexandra Edmonds, for her loving support, her insatiable curiosity, and her infectious zest for life. She is a natural repotter.

INDEX

ABOUT THE AUTHOR

FRANCES EDMONDS has had an extraordinary professional career full of transitions and transformation, latterly becoming a longevity and well-being fellow at Stanford University's Distinguished Careers Institute in 2018, where the concept of "repotting" was born. She is an inspirational keynote speaker, a cross-generational mentor, and a cocreator of the UK's most prestigious business development network. Previously an international conference interpreter at the European Union, United Nations, and World Economic Summits, she is also a bestselling author and broadcaster. She divides her time between London and the South of France.

francesedmonds.co.uk